THE STORY OF TOMMY

RICHARD BARNES & PETE TOWNSHEND

Published by Eel Pie Publishing Ltd.
The Boathouse, Ranelagh Drive, Twickenham
Middlesex TW1 1QZ
England

ISBN 0 906008 02 6 (Hardback edition)
ISBN 0 906008 01 8 (Paperback edition)

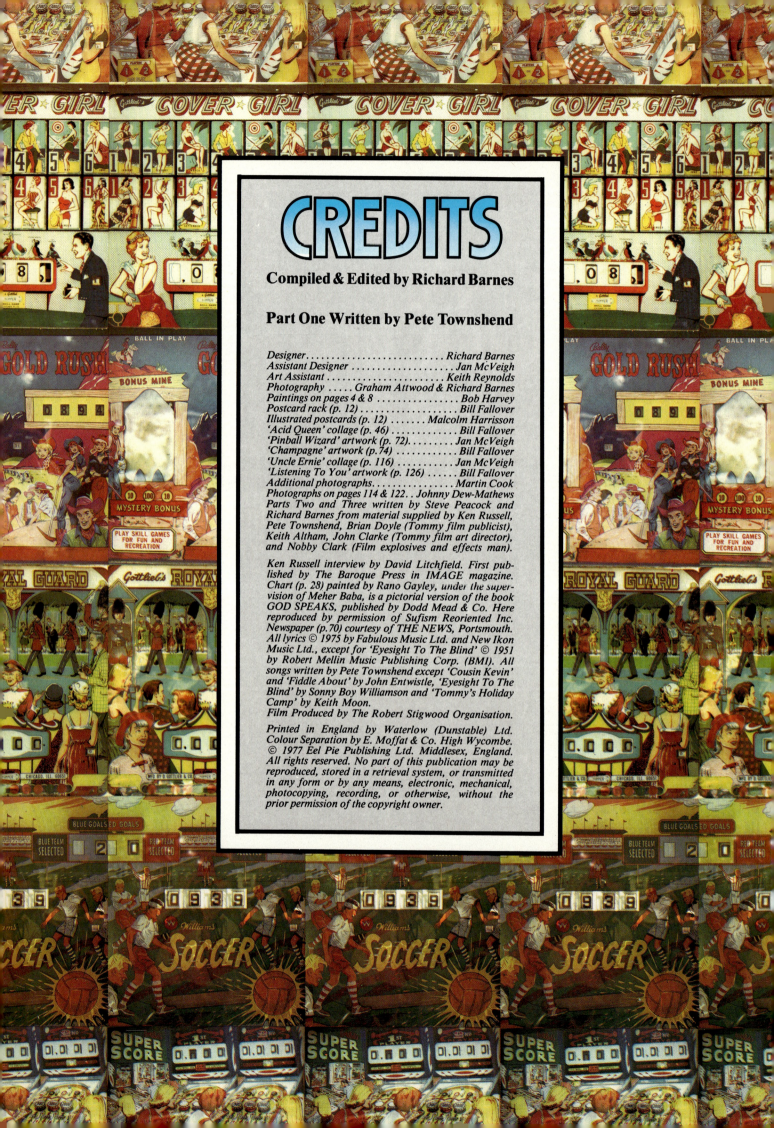

CREDITS

Compiled & Edited by Richard Barnes

Part One Written by Pete Townshend

Designer............................Richard Barnes
Assistant Designer ....Jan McVeigh
Art Assistant ....Keith Reynolds
Photography ..... Graham Attwood & Richard Barnes
Paintings on pages 4 & 8 .... Bob Harvey
Postcard rack (p. 12) .... Bill Fallover
Illustrated postcards (p. 12) .... Malcolm Harrisson
'Acid Queen' collage (p. 46) .... Bill Fallover
'Pinball Wizard' artwork (p. 72)......... Jan McVeigh
'Champagne' artwork (p.74) .... Bill Fallover
'Uncle Ernie' collage (p. 116) .... Jan McVeigh
'Listening To You' artwork (p. 126) ...... Bill Fallover
Additional photographs................. Martin Cook
Photographs on pages 114 & 122 .. Johnny Dew-Mathews
Parts Two and Three written by Steve Peacock and Richard Barnes from material supplied by Ken Russell, Pete Townshend, Brian Doyle (Tommy film publicist), Keith Altham, John Clarke (Tommy film art director), and Nobby Clark (Film explosives and effects man).

Ken Russell interview by David Litchfield. First published by The Baroque Press in IMAGE magazine. Chart (p. 28) painted by Rano Gayley, under the supervision of Meher Baba, is a pictorial version of the book GOD SPEAKS, published by Dodd Mead & Co. Here reproduced by permission of Sufism Reoriented Inc. Newspaper (p.70) courtesy of THE NEWS, Portsmouth. All lyrics © 1975 by Fabulous Music Ltd. and New Ikon Music Ltd., except for 'Eyesight To The Blind' © 1951 by Robert Mellin Music Publishing Corp. (BMI). All songs written by Pete Townshend except 'Cousin Kevin' and 'Fiddle About' by John Entwistle, 'Eyesight To The Blind' by Sonny Boy Williamson and 'Tommy's Holiday Camp' by Keith Moon.
Film Produced by The Robert Stigwood Organisation.

Printed in England by Waterlow (Dunstable) Ltd.
Colour Separation by E. Moffat & Co. High Wycombe.
© 1977 Eel Pie Publishing Ltd. Middlesex, England.
All rights reserved. No part of this publication may be reproduced, stored in a retrieval system, or transmitted in any form or by any means, electronic, mechanical, photocopying, recording, or otherwise, without the prior permission of the copyright owner.

CONTENTS

Part One/Writing Tommy 4

Part Two/Filming Tommy 34

Part Three/Tommy People 86

Ken Russell 86
Roger Daltrey 100
Ann-Margret 104
Oliver Reed 106
Pete Townshend 110

Part Four/Tommy Lyrics 8

(Part Four consists of pages of illustrated lyrics made up from, or inspired by, images from the TOMMY movie and placed in sequence throughout the book)

Captain Walker 8
It's A Boy 9
Bernie's Holiday Camp 12, 13, 14
1951/What About The Boy? 15, 16, 17
Amazing Journey 20, 21
Christmas 24, 25
Eyesight To The Blind 38, 39, 40, 41
Acid Queen 46, 47
Do You Think It's Alright/Cousin Kevin ... 62, 63
Do You Think It's Alright/Fiddle About ... 68, 69
Pinball Wizard 72, 73, 75
Champagne 74, 75
There's A Doctor 84
Go To The Mirror 85
Tommy Can You Hear Me? 90
Smash The Mirror 91
I'm Free 94, 95
Mother And Son 98
Sensation 99
Sally Simpson 102, 103
Welcome 108
T.V. Studio 109
Tommy's Holiday Camp 116, 117
We're Not Gonna Take It! 120, 121
See Me, Feel Me 124, 125
Listening To You 126, 127

PART ONE/WRITING TOMMY

"The boy is incredibly withdrawn.", said the doctor,"As far as I can make out, his long life as a bedridden child has affected a total coma. I've known cases of this when patients remain in this deep sleep for years." Mother looked at father, and father looked at mother, they both would resign themselves to this new sadness quickly it was clear, they had faced twelve long years of tension up till now, waiting for their son to recover from his semi trance like state which had kept him from them, amd another two or fifty years would not make any difference now. "I suggest you allow a nurse to instruct you how to feed the lad and so on," the doctor wen t on, "The better health he is in, the more chance there is that he will stay outof his coma permanantly when he does awaken."

I could hear it all. It was faint and even slightly reverberant in my head, I heard my father talk to me, he would talk to me often, obviously not believin gthat any of his words were getting through but talking to me none-the-less. He always talked rubbish, nothing I could have understood even if I'd have known him. In fact I knew nothing. I was always too deep in withdrawl to take education, and the only words ever spoken to me were the curses of the nurses who had to take me to the lavatory. But I could hear them. All of them, all the time, yet it was impossible for me to know what they meant when thay said,"He cant hear a word we are saying!", for I couldnt even distinguish between the spoken word and odd noises in the room, they all sounded so natural, all arrived as simple vibrations of the air. I hadnt left that room since I was brought home from hospital at seventeen months, Aware of everything I could not translate or understand anything I heard or saw or felt. I couldnt co-ordinate the muscles of my body to move, or even move them to co-ordinate them, I was just aware of being aware so to speak, solid, and non active. But this recent developement shocked me, even in my delerium. One night, as I lay allowing the barrage of information being fed to me by my senses to wash over me in a kind of sleep, I found myself suddenly able to do something. What I could do wasnt a lot, but it was an incredible sensatio for me, as I had never regarded my senses as mine to regard or my body mine to control, I found I had the ability to stem my senses flow to my brain. Of course, already in an amzingly complete neutrality I would have preferred some kind of active event, but this was huge anyway.I had the power, the power, the power, to stop the barrage, the unending, incessant bombardment of my soul by these relentless stimulii. So I did, slowly at first, but then faster and faster as I grew used to my new talent. Each tiny change in conciousness was a revelation to me, so green to any kind of change at all during my childhood years. And now I had finally reached complete peace, complete quiet, complete freedom from the ignorance tha could not allow me to see order in the chaos my body presented me.At least nearly. Itseemed that the further I got nto non thought, the more effort was required to take me further, and so each time the moment came for me to completely pass away from all the cloudy, distant, but obvious stimulii, I became suddenly aware of some difficulty. It was like trying to commit suicide without a weapon, I had no weapon, only the powers of withdrawl, each time I came near the blissful peace of non existence some crude and compelling life force hurled me back.

"Tommy" has passed through many stages in its lifetime: A mere idea, an uncomplicated dream, an unsuccessful study of orchestration, a Hesse-like novel ... hundreds of variations.

What is enclosed here is where we are at today. I daren't say this is the definitive version of Tommy. Many people more attached to the Who's album than Ken Russell's film would no doubt object. Even people who loved the film might feel that Tommy could easily be improved on or even edited down to a simpler basis.

I think it would be very interesting to look at all the stages of Tommy's history from my point of view, as the main writer and composer. To look at the whole thing now might be indulgent, at a time when things are by no means over for the film. But there is a new interest in Tommy now, and many people think of it purely as an idea or gimmick; the brainchild of some rock musician with pretensions of grandeur.

Strangely enough, writing Tommy was something that simultaneously brought me as a composer, tremendous praise and criticism. Many fans of The Who and of rock in general have never been able to see where an 'opera' fits alongside songs like "My Generation", or "Substitute". In a sense, Tommy really does form a tremendous part of my retrospective writing output. Such a lot of time and energy went into it, so many ideas, and more specifically so many actual songs were used in Tommy. Sometimes they were used up, changed about from original songs intended for other purposes, or written specially for the opera, then ditched.

Writing rock songs was something I *ended up* doing. When I was young I thought of myself as a Rock Star rather than a rock writer. I would dress in front of a mirror, standing with a guitar, legs apart, trying to look like one of "The Shadows". I wrote a couple of songs for The Who when they were called "The Detours" back around 1960. My first song to be published was called "It Was You" and was recorded by a Beatle-ish group called "The Naturals" in 1963. Needless to say it was a flop. It could even have been a B-side, I can't really remember. I just remember showing up at art college having visited the publisher, full of talk of 'advances' and 'really big money'.

When later, The Who took their first serious record company audition, we were turned down because we didn't, at that time, play any original material. It seemed obvious that I should try to write, having had some experience, and I began a song called "Can't Explain", which was in the charts about six weeks after I'd written it. Things moved fast in those days. I didn't really feel serious about songwriting, although I did admire serious non 'pop' writers like Dylan and Nina Simone. What made me become serious was the fact that I discovered that I really could communicate far more honestly and effectively through music than through conversation or relationships.

What I learned was, that I could write a song about anything, absolutely anything, and something quite surprising and candid would emerge between the lines of an ostensibly simple song. Even I didn't really understand how this happened, but to the public of course this was 'talent' – later 'genius'. I would love to be able to say it was just 'hard work'. Often the harder I worked at something, the less real and connected with its audience (and my own life), it seemed to be. So I knew that Tommy would have to be on an unconscious basis. I would have to form a hard core on which to build songs that I hadn't written specifically for an opera. So I looked through my notes, my sheets and sheets of unused words, and discovered several songs; the songs that served as the hard core of Tommy.

I thought about the American tour in 1967 when the Who used to do two-hour long performances of old-time hit material when we toured with Herman's Hermits. At that time after each show performing numbers like the "Mini Opera", "Substitute", "Happy Jack", "Pictures of Lily", "Little Billy", and songs of this type. I used to rush back to the hotel room to work, writing songs or collating lyrics, or scribbling out ideas for the opera that I was working on at the time called "Amazing Journey". More about that later.

On another occasion in America, I remember a performance at the Fillmore West in San Francisco, where after playing and playing and playing, deep into the night, again probably a two or three hour show, Jann Wenner, who is the editor of Rolling Stone Magazine, invited me back for a long interview at his home. I described to him in some depth, the 'vision', if you like (although it does make it sound pompous, but at the time it was just a vision, nothing had exactly been done), of the story of Tommy, and of the idea, the concept.

(The following is an extract from this interview, originally printed in Rolling Stone magazine dated September 14th. 1968 and carried over to the following issue).

What other ideas in this field do you have?

Well, the album concept in general is complex. I don't

Pete finalized his ideas for Tommy during this interview.

know if I can explain it in my condition, at the moment. But it's derived as a result of quite a few things. We've been talking about doing an opera; we've been talking about doing like albums, we've been talking about a whole lot of things, and what has basically happened is that we've condensed all of these ideas, all this energy and all these gimmicks, and whatever we've decided on for future albums, into one juicy package. The package I hope is going to be called "Deaf, Dumb and Blind Boy." It's a story about a kid that's born deaf, dumb and blind and what happens to him throughout his life. The deaf, dumb and blind boy is played by The Who, the musical entity. He's represented musically, represented by a theme which we play, which starts off the opera itself and then there's a song describing the deaf, dumb and blind boy. But what it's really all about is the fact that because the boy is "D, D & B," he's seeing things basically as vibrations which we translate to music. That's really what we want to do: create this feeling that when you listen to the music you can actually become aware of the boy, and aware of what he is all about, because we are creating him as we play.

Yes, it's a pretty far out thing actually. But it's very, very endearing to me because the thing is . . . inside, the boy sees things musically and in dreams and nothing has got any weight at all. He is touched from the outside and he feels his mother's touch, he feels his father's touch, but he just interprets them as music. His father gets pretty upset that his kid is deaf, dumb and blind. He wants a kid that will play football and God knows what.

One night he comes in and he's drunk and he sits over the kid's bed and looks at him and he starts to talk to him, and the kid just smiles up, and his father is trying to get through to him, telling him about how the other dads have a kid that they can take to football and they can teach them to play football and all this kind of crap and he starts to say, "Can you hear me?" The kid, of course, can't hear him. He's groovin' in this musical thing, this incredible musical thing, he'll be out of his mind. Then there's his father outside, outside of his body, and this

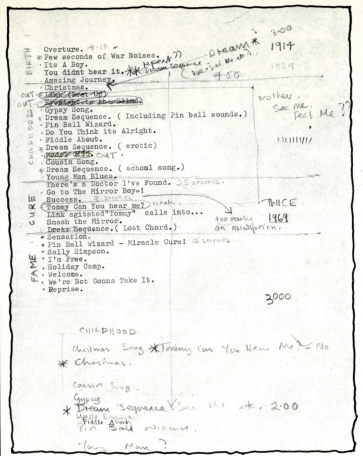

List showing sequence of songs, prior to recording Tommy.

song is going to be written by John. I hope John will write this song about the father who is really uptight now.

The kid won't respond, he just smiles. The father starts to hit him and at this moment the whole thing becomes incredibly realistic. On one side you have the dreamy music of the boy wasting through his nothing life. And on the other you have the reality of the father outside, uptight, but now you've got blows, you've got communication. The father is hitting the kid; musically then I want the thing to break out, hand it over to Keith—"this is your scene, man, take it from here."

And the kid doesn't catch the violence. He just knows that some sensation is happening. He doesn't feel the pain, he doesn't associate it with anything. He just accepts it.

A similar situation happens later on in the opera, where the father starts to get the mother to take the kid away from home to an uncle. The uncle is a bit of a perv, you know. He plays with the kid's body while the kid is out. And at this particular time the child has heard his own name, his mother called him. And he managed to hear these words: "Tommy". He's really got this big thing about his name, whatever his name is going to be, you know "Tommy". And he gets really hung-up on his own name. He decides that this is the king and this is the goal. Tommy is the thing, man.

He's going through this and the uncle comes in and starts to go through a scene with the kid's body, you know, and the boy experiences sexual vibrations, you know, sexual experience, and again it's just basic music, it's interpreted as music and it is nothing more than music. It's got no association with sleeziness or with undercover or with any of the things normally associated with sex. None of the romance, none of the visual stimulus, none of the sound stimulus. Just basic touch. It's meaningless. Or not meaningless, you just don't react, you know. Slowly but surely the kid starts to get it together, out of this simplicity, this incredible simplicity in his mind. He starts to realize that he can see and he can hear, and he can speak; they are there and they are happening all the time. And that all the time he has been able to hear and see. All the time it's been there in front of him, for him to see.

This is the difficult jump. It's going to be extremely difficult, but we want to try to do it musically. At this point, the theme, which has been the boy, starts to change. You start to realize that he is coming to the point where he is going to get over the top, he's going to get over his hang-ups. You're gonna stop monkeying around with songs about people being tinkered with, and with father's getting uptight, with mother's getting precious and things, and you're gonna get down to the fact of what is going to happen to the kid.

The music has got to explain what happens, that the boy elevates, and finds something which is incredible. To us, it's nothing to be able to see and hear and speak, but to him, it's absolutely incredible and overwhelming; this is what we want to do musically. Lyrically, it's quite easy to do it, in fact I've written it out several times. It makes great poetry, but so much depends on the music, so much. I'm hoping that we can do it. The lyrics are going to be okay, but every pitfall of what we're trying to say lies in the music, lies in the way we play the music, the way we interpret, the way things are going during the opera.

The main characters are going to be the boy, and his musical things, he's got a mother and father and an uncle. There is a doctor involved who tries to do some psychiatric treatment on the kid which is only partly successful. The first two big events are when he hears his mother calling him and hears the word, "Tommy" and he devotes a whole part of his life to this one word. The second important event is when he sees himself in a mirror, suddenly seeing himself for the first time: he takes an immediate back step, bases his whole life around his own image. The whole thing then becomes incredibly introverted. The music and the lyrics become introverted and he starts to talk about himself, starts to talk about his beauty. Not knowing, of course, that what he saw was him, but still regarding it as something which belonged to him, and of course it did all of the time anyway.

It's a very complex thing and I don't know if I'm getting it across.
You are.
Because I don't feel at all together.
I know you don't look it, but you're coming on very together.
Good.

In my first notes I talked of an opera that would tell a spiritual story in a parallel way, from the inside and from the outside, (see notes) but the solid undercurrent riding through all the material was the fact that I was in a 'newfound spiritual mood'. When looking through my past notes for material for this article I found prayers to Meher Baba. I don't remember praying much before that date, but I do believe in the power of prayer. I'm not going to qualify that statement, there are too many diverse ways to God, people are too delicate about the rightness of their own chosen path. (Don't want to feel they could be wasting their time you know).

Some of the prayers I wrote to Meher Baba became lyrics of songs.

For example, Baba – When my fist clenches . . . . crack it open.

I had lost my temper with a groupie, who on my arrival at Denver presented me with a bottle of C.C. and maybe even herself (I should be so lucky). But I threw her out. I got a little worried that that wasn't the way to do things and wrote the above prayer which I later used in the bridge of "Behind Blue Eyes". Incidentally, later that night in the same hotel, I was awakened by a small group of White Panthers who had come to violently avenge Abbie Hoffman, whom I threw offstage at Woodstock. I came very, very close to getting my head cracked open when I lost my temper with them, (they were quite small people), then a giant emerged from the

CAPTAIN WALKER

Captain Walker
Didn't come home
His unborn child
Will never know him
He's believed
to be missing
With a number of men
Don't expect
To see him again

IT'S A BOY

It's a boy, Mrs. Walker,
it's a boy
It's a boy, Mrs. Walker,
it's a boy
A son! A son! A son!
Hear the joyful celebrations
in the streets
It's a boy born on this
first day of peace
We've won! A son!
We've won!

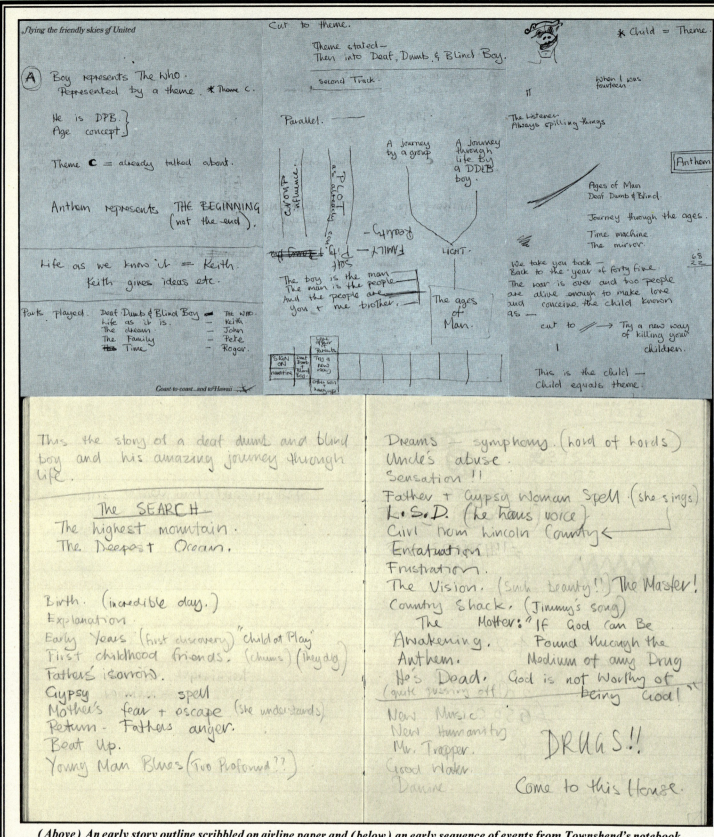

(Above) An early story outline scribbled on airline paper and (below) an early sequence of events from Townshend's notebook.

shadows in the hallway. He was big, black, hated me, and he called me chicken shit. Such is life that I ran for it. Sometimes I blamed Meher Baba, even in a prayer for my being down.

'You teach me to forgive, and I am learning,
Oh Master.'
Forgive my sloth and lethargy,
You pattern my talent, prescribe my doom.
A gloom more terrifying than my dull mind is capable of imagining.

Much of my early spiritual focus, before I heard of Meher Baba, was tempered by my reading of the Spaceship sagas of George Adamski. He had said that on another planet in our system existed a race of people who were spiritually perfect. He claimed that he was in contact with them. While reading the books I believed this, somehow this man taught me to open my mind. In other words he taught me faith. The first few prayers to Meher Baba contained extracts from what he said he had been told by these spacemen. They talked of The Divine Presence, The Divine Intelligence, The Divine Awareness. Meher Baba talked of Infinite Power, Infinite Knowledge and Infinite Bliss.

OH FATHER: PARVARDIGAR BABA=LOVE

You are the DIVINE PRESENCE
You are the DIVINE AWARENESS
You are the DIVINE INTELLIGENCE
Oh Baba, Lover of my soul,
You taught me before I even knew of Your Presence.
You awoke me,
Via every pair of lips.
From them Your words flowed,
From every book Your knowledge poured,
From every event we learn another of
Your lessons, YOU called.

Divine and most merciful.
You *only* have the POWER, KNOWLEDGE and BLISS.
Via YOU I will love You more.
Fully and totally.
Even as I loved myself BEFORE YOU.

Incredibly, this honeymoon with prayer was short-lived. I say incredibly because as I said earlier, I believe in the power of prayer. I believe simply because at that time it worked. It pulled me together; I looked at myself and my motives and amassed my work and really got down to writing Tommy.

I had dithered tremendously with the previous opera I had tried to write. That was called "Rael", and I intended it to be written for full orchestra and to be a genuine opera. Looking back, I can't quite remember where The Who as a group fitted in, because I had Arthur Brown lined up as the hero. I always thought Arthur's manic voice, and the way it zoomed from classical vibrato to screaming Jay Hawkins was a perfect foil for a Rock Opera.

"Rael" was politically based thematically, perhaps that's why it flopped even before it began. I'm not a great political head. The story was about the year 1999 (not as cliched as 2000 you see) and the emergence of the Red

(continued)
I will be a greencoat too
And when I'm big I'll own a holiday camp
A camp with a difference
Always be good weather
When you come to Tommy's
The holiday's forever
I'm glad you like your Uncle Frank
He'll surely love you too
Just like a Dad
He's very nice I think
Did *he* fight in the war?
When he's got his greencoat on
I love him even more

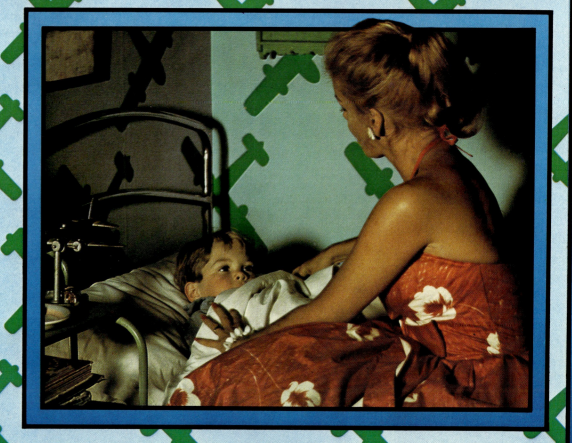

Got a feeling fifty one
Is going to be a good year
Especially if you and me
See it out together

So you think that fifty one
Is going to be a good year
We'll marry now and
See it out together

I have no reason to be
over optimistic
But somehow when you smile
I can brave bad weather

WHAT ABOUT THE BOY?

Chinese (The Redchins) as world leaders. The only spiritual note was that the Redchins were regarded as being fairly evil because they were crushing the old established religions as they conquered. Again, looking back, I think maybe that isn't such a bad thing.

"Rael" resembled the later "Quadrophenia" in some ways, in fact both "Rael" and Tommy and the later aborted Life House contained various similarities of theme and purpose. They all started as vehicles for the group, so the individual characters in the group all influenced the characters I'd invented, very deeply.

In 1966, at my studio in Wardour Street I wrote this (one of the first idea-sheets for "Rael"):—

"Opening is set at sea. In order to create a wide linear feeling in the opening of the opera. The sound of the sea in deep echo is heard. It must be fairly artificial so as not to start too heavily.
NARRATOR SINGING. Someone, a man, is leaving home, (thoughts of home). He is wealthy. He has broken many ties. It is a time of indecision. He is on a boat that recently left harbour and is heading out to sea. He wonders if he is doing right."

The temptation toward self-analysis is enormous here, but I'll leave all that to you. Basically the story was running into about twenty scenes when Kit Lambert reminded me that while I was pretending to be Wagner, The Who needed a new single. What did I have? I had "Rael". Thus Rael was edited down to four minutes (too long for a single in those days ironically) and recorded in New York for that purpose. It later appeared on an album. No-one will ever know what it means, it has been squeezed up too tightly to make sense. Musically it is interesting because it contains a theme which I later used in Tommy for "Sparks" and the "Underture". That music was written in 1966.

An interesting point on the side was that the hero, named Damon after our then recording engineer (I thought his name was romantic) had a lisp. I admitted in one of the sheets that it had no bearing on the plot, but it does throw some light on why Tommy turned out to be deaf, dumb and blind. I always loved circus and freaks, and the only group I ever produced, Thunderclap Newman, was another expression of this love of freaks who make it. The fallen raised up. I also nearly produced Tiny Tim.

In 1967 I moved to my wife's flat in Victoria and later to Lower Belgravia (Ebury Street) where Tommy began to take shape. LSD had come and gone by then. During the year I was taking acid I wrote hardly anything, probably the most revealing testimony to its uselessness I ever experienced, although the images I saw still influence my music. I had a studio at Ebury Street on the top floor. I had nice big playback speakers at the time, and as usual when writing I would prepare demos (test recordings of the songs) before I even played them to the group or even suggested to the group that there might be the possibility of a song. One of the reasons I still find to this day the need to make a recording of a song myself, is that songwriting to me (and probably to everyone) is a very impulsive process and a very revealing process. One has to be very careful that one doesn't say anything that one is going to regret at a later date. Making tapes, complete tapes in fact, you don't just have an idea whether a song is good, you also know whether it is going to be possible to complete it. You get some glimpse as to how best it will be arranged. Perhaps in the process of sorting it out at home, adding instruments – adding organ, drums or bass to a simple guitar part – you'd get the feeling. Maybe you even make a mistake, and so at least one of the many infinite possibilities would be dealt with. The most fascinating thing about this recording studio in particular, was that it was the room in which Tommy – the first few songs from Tommy were born. I worked pretty much when I liked, and the sound didn't seem to disturb any neighbours. In the same house, down

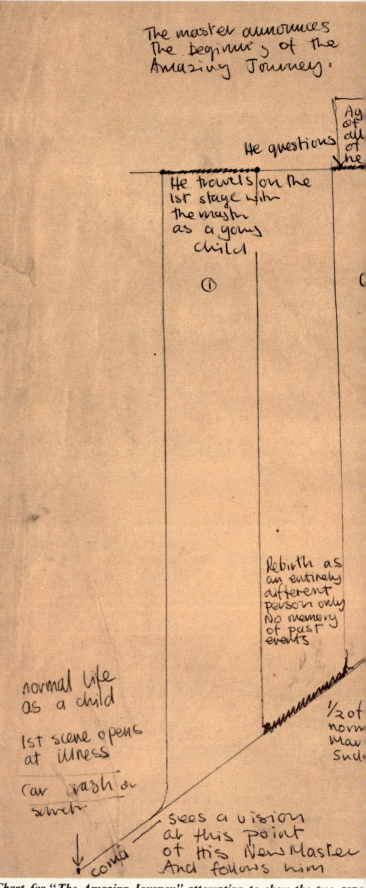

Chart for "The Amazing Journey" attempting to show the two aspe

in the basement, lived an elderly but quiet couple, who didn't ever complain. In my studio I had a drum kit, an organ, an electric piano, two old Revox stereo tape recorders, a rather ancient but well made microphone mixer, and some odd effects that I used to use to enhance my recordings – limiters, and some echo and so on and so forth.

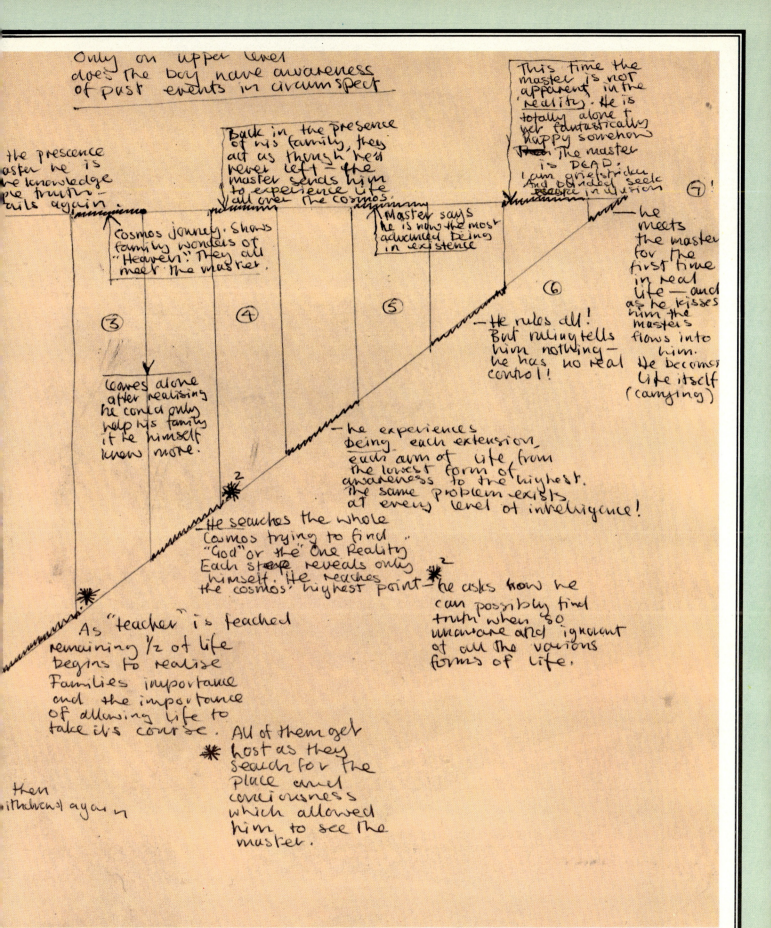

living. The aspect of Reality and the aspect of Illusion. Townshend later adopted a more fluid framework and dropped this complex structure.

After LSD and flying saucers I became more deeply immersed in Meher Baba through contact with other people who were following Him, mainly, Mike McInnerney and his wife Katie. The contact with Mike was the most important really, although others I loved strengthened me at the time (like Ronnie Lane for example). Mike's appreciation and reaction to the Tommy ideas kept me moving when the thing was under way. I was playing him tapes so that he could get the feel of the thing to do the album-cover artwork. I remember making a tape of the basic chords for "Welcome", a song I wrote, much to the alarm of Richard Stanley, a friend of mine who was then living with us. I was really writing the song about what I felt was an emotion that was actually in my life at the

WHO'S PETE—SICK OR TRUTHFUL?

I HOPE the public will not be conned into keeping quiet about "Tommy," by that much over-used phrase "sickness is in the mind of the listener."

WHO'S SICK OPERA

THE WHO: TOMMY (Track stereo 613 013/4; 75s 1d)

I REALLY was looking forward to this "pop opera," which occupied Pete Townshend's mind for so long. Really I w But what a disappointment, even though I tip it for the NME charts.

Admittedly the idea is original, even though other groups seem to be jumping on the bandwagon now, but it doesn't come off. Running for over an hour, it goes on and on and isn't totally representative of the Who; maybe it's time for a change in style, but if this is it, I long for a return to the old days.

Beautifully packaged in a tri-fold out sleeve, the double album also includes a twelve-page brochure containing the words of the songs and pictures to illustrate the numbers.

Pretentious is too strong a word; maybe over-ambitious is the right term but sick certainly does apply. One line goes "Sickness will surely take the mind." It does. **RG.**

Tracks: Overture, It's A Boy, 1921, Amazing Journey, Sparks, The Hawker, Christmas, Cousin Kevin, The Acid Queen, Underture Do You Think It's Alright, Fiddle About, Pinball Wizard, There's A Doctor, Go To The Mirror, Tommy Can You Hear Me, Smash The Mirror Sensation, Miracle Cure,

Birth of the first rock opera

Is this man sick?

'PINBALL WIZARD' STORM: BACK PA

Who says 'Tommy' is sick, Auntie?

time; a feeling that I was becoming a part of some state of mind, some state of reference that I had never experienced before, and it was something I simply wanted to share. I put this to words, in a very sort of trite way in a sense, in the shape of "Welcome". One evening I asked Richard Stanley up to my studio to play in the song. He was deeply embarrassed, because he misconstrued the words where I say, "Come to this house, and be one of the comfortable people, come to this house and be one of us", as an open invitation to him from my wife and I to engage in some, I suppose, co-habitation. I don't really know, anyway he was very embarrassed at the time and said so. Richard was another of the bouncing boards for many of my ideas regarding the early Tommy. I was full of mystical feelings, but Richard, though a great friend, was less interested in Meher Baba than in the music I was coming up with. When I showed him a piece of paper with two lines that embodied the original Tommy theme (an event he still talks about today) he seemed pretty confused. When I look at it today, I feel the same way. The two lines were meant to represent the two aspects of the way we live our lives – the two viewpoints: One the aspect of illusion and the other the aspect of reality. The fact that we grope our way through our lives believing everything we see to be real, but in fact it is an illusion. and that the reality is a mystical thing, a hidden thing, and something the essence of which only comes to us slowly and painfully through experience, and experience is a timeless and everlasting thing – or so I thought at the time.

My idea was, that I would write a series of songs that flashed between the point of view of reality and the point of view of illusion, seen through the eyes of someone on the spiritual path, a young boy, and I called the basic idea "Amazing Journey". It was sometime later when the idea struck me that having a two-pronged concept was very cumbersome. Having to have one song about what was really happening to a person, and another song about what appeared to be happening, was too much of an oscillatory way of going about things. I had to find some way of making the illusion of life organic and graspable by someone listening to the story.

The hero, still unnamed in 1968, was to begin his operatic career by dying in a car crash. I could go on for hours about what led up to the hero's immortalisation as Tommy, but perhaps a look at those early notes would tell all. I already had written songs which were to become, "Welcome", "Not Gonna Take It", "Sensation", and "Sparks" and "The Underture". But, when the songs that I wrote before Tommy were brought together as an idea, they didn't really have any meaning out of context, and it was only later, when I brought them together as part of Tommy, that I saw their meaning. This might sound a bit peculiar, but obviously a songwriter is just

Who's 'Tommy' – a masterpiece

THE NEW LPs

THE WHO "Tommy." It's A Boy; 1921; Amazing Journey; Sparks; The Hawker; Christmas; Cousin Kevin; The Acid Queen; Do You Think It's Alright; Fiddle About; Pinball

Pinball man Pete knows his score

WHO OPERA AT COLISEUM

And Now a Rock Opera!

Who triumph at the home of opera

Is the New Rock Opera a Breakthrough?

one person. When I write something today, I might write about the standard lamp that I see in front of me, I might write about the kids I hear shouting in the street. Whatever I write about will *come* from me (obviously), my mind and the way that I am, it will come from a point in my evolution, upwards or downwards. At a later date, looking back, it will fall neatly into place. This is what happened to so many of the songs from Tommy. "Sensation", for example, was another song I wrote before Tommy, and I wrote it about a girl that I felt had a tremendous spiritual presence. At that time the lyric was "She's a Sensation", rather than the later "He's a Sensation". But again this was something, if you like, that serves as an example of my thinking in spiritual terms, rather than the frustrated adolescent terms I had been thinking in, up to that point. "We're not Gonna Take It", the whole finale of Tommy (excluding "Listening To You, I Get The Music", which was composed at a much later date), was again something written before Tommy had actually been formed as a total idea, and that particular song wasn't about Tommy's devotees at all – it was about the rabble in general, that rabble out there; the consensus rabble; how we, myself as part of them, were not going to take fascism, we're not going to take dreary, dying politics; were not going to take things the way they were, the way they always had been and that we were keen to change things.

"Eyesight to the Blind", I incorporated, because it actually mentioned the words, deaf, dumb, and blind, in it, and then it turned out to be quite fundamental to the whole idea. The whole concept of "Holiday Camp" was something that came up much much later toward the end of the recording session, and Keith suggested that the whole thing be set in a Holiday Camp and I picked up on that. As we were leaving IBC studios one day, I said to Keith and John as they were walking down the stairs, "I've really got to do something with this whole business of the 'establishment', the 'church', or what turns out to be the 'church' at the end of the story. I've got to work out something to give it life, to make it real, to make it palatable, but not something churchy, which would make the whole tone of the album pretentious". Keith said, "Well I've been thinking that it would be a good idea to set the whole thing in a Holiday Camp". I said, "What a great idea", and Keith said, "Well O.K. I'll write that tonight". I thought, "God Almighty, if Keith goes off and gets into writing songs about Holiday Camps, I don't know how they're ever going to fit in". So I said to him, "Don't worry Keith, I've already written it". I think he took my point, because he didn't actually write anything that night, and when I got home I wrote the short piece called "Ernies Holiday Camp". Keith got the credit for it because it was his idea, and also I felt, it turned out just as he himself would have written it.

23

Did you ever see
the faces of the children
They get so excited
Waking up on Christmas morning
Hours before
the winter sun's ignited
They believe in dreams
and all they mean
Including heaven's generosity
Peeping round the door to see
what parcels are for free
In curiosity
And Tommy doesn't know
what day it is
He doesn't know who Jesus was
or what praying is

How can he be saved?
From the eternal grave

Tommy can you hear me?
Tommy can you hear me?
Tommy can you hear me?
Tommy can you hear me?
Tommy can you hear me?
How can he be saved?

*See me, feel me,
touch me, heal me
See me, feel me,
touch me, heal me*

Tommy can you hear me?
Tommy can you hear me?
How can he be saved?

Surrounded by his friends
He sits so silently and unaware of anything
Glazy eyed he picks his nose
He smiles he cries
He pokes his tongue at everything

I believe in love
But how can men
who've never seen light, be enlightened?
Only if he's cured
Will his spirit's future level ever heighten

And Tommy doesn't know what day it is
He doesn't know who Jesus was or what praying is

How can he be saved?
From the eternal grave?

Glow Girl.

Separates and lingerie
Seven pairs of shoes
Lots of Woolworth's make-up
And a dozen pairs o' trues

The wing of the airplane
Is just caught on fire
I ~~say~~ without reservations
We ain't going no higher

~~Seven~~ Five or six stories all
ending up somewhere.

Twelve campus sweatshirts
A thousand photographs
A million little memories
A million laughs.

The plane is diving faster
We're getting near the ground
I'd expected some screaming
But there ain't a sound.

My old piano
My yellow bike
My dirty habits
TV. shows I like

It's nearly over
I can't complain
I've had some good times
And I'll be round again.

~~DIVE~~ EXPLOSION.

So this is the place
Wow
One mind
One body
One thought
One direction
One feeling
One muscle
One ~~love~~ erection.

The Father has taken the boy to the
Doctor and is trying to explain the boy's
peculiar presence. and vibrations.

DOCTOR He seems to be completely unreceptive.
The tests I gave him came to naught at all
But there is certainly something undetected
Though he's quiet, I somehow hear him call

BOY See Me. Feel Me. Touch Me. Heal Me.

FATHER I kicked him licked him rubbed him hit him
Loved him
Everything I've tried to let him know
I'm here my son You Don't I wait for
And in my brain frustration overflows—   you want

BOY See Me. Feel Me. Touch Me. Heal Me.

DOCTOR There is a chance.

FATHER Nevertheless I feel it must be done
For what is life to him as he is now
The beauty ~~is~~ of the world is
all escaping.
If ~~he could see what he sees hundred~~
~~cover~~

~~Nevertheless~~
For ~~what from Coast to Coast~~ it should be done
For what is life to him as he is now
Empty of the beauty of the sun
And silent as the ~~oceans~~ floors — but how?

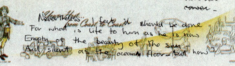

There is a chance — a recent operation
Was successful on a boy with same co-
But he was accustomed to shock and co
The thing is — from the darkness to
of the world is

To successfully jump the gap it takes a

There is a chance — an untried operati
But remember just how shocked you
When after twenty years of total da
He suddenly can hear and speak a

I often wonder what he's feeli
~~What too thirsty and how to do~~
~~Is there an~~ Has he heard a word
I ~~his~~ his fumbling touch appeals
What is happening in his he

Father
Interpolated between mother song.

Gone!!!
Gone !!!???**

Well find them you fools
And quickly I'm warning
My wife must have taken him
Early this morning.
(quieter)
Please dearest the boy
Please don't destroy
This chance is just once
In a lifetime
The planets are right
Their positions tonight
Will ~~never~~ ever return
Bef—

Where are you my wife
Must you play with his life
Our son could be cured
And be near us
Instead of so distant
Remote and resistant
Never sees, never speaks
cannot hear us.

Oh Tommy to walk with you
Out in the park
Pushing your swing
Watching stars in the dark
To watch your face light up
'S I appear when you're frightened
To see you excited
To ~~see~~ ~~you~~ enlightened

Deaf, Dumb & Blind boys
Mother can't take the decision
changes into husband - and in
a moment of panic leaves
taking the boy with her.

If only you knew what was
happening to you
You'd be grateful your mother
was taking you too
Away from your dad and his
electrical table

If only you knew
What could happen to you
You would shake like leaf
in a storm
For your father is crazy
And as he experiments
He alters what nature has born

I'm not religious
But his plan is hideous
Doctors who warn him he scorns

And soon little son
What God has begun
Will end we must leave before
dawn.

continued
a few pages on

```
Hey policeman dont you like my music?
I give it to you.
I know you collect my records
I love you too.
So dont pretend you cant see me as I really am.
Justify then set me free
Try to change the plan
Cause we dont have to take it,
Never did and never will
We dont have to take it,
Gonna break it,
Better shake it,
Lets forget it better still!

Those ladies wearin wigs and hairnets
Theyer looking cool
Isee some Bermuda shorts that dont break one rule,
I'm not a law breaker either,
Dont know no laws,
And since I wasnt there when you made them,
I got one more...
We dont have to take it..

I travelled to New York on thursday, they know me there.
Wednesday we hit Kansas and the barman wouldnt give me beer.
On Tuesday we got back to London, no bettr I fear!
For a young man is a stung man if he dont lend his ear.
etc.

Hey you getting drunk in Charlies, I've got you sussed.
Hey you gettin stoned at a party, this is a bust
Hey hung up old mister normal dont try to gain my trust
Cos I dont do it none of your ways, though think I must!

You say I dont propose no answers, just break things down,
But they aint my questions youre puttin round
Just look at me and my brothers, look at our smiling way,
For you lost us at sunday school and the Lord gained us today!
Were not gonna take it
Nothing will be said
We dont have to tak it
Didnt make it, better rake it, commmon take it from your head.

We dont have to take it from you or anyone,
We aint gonna take it gonna break it no mistaking
It shall be done.

I aint no high-nose, but youre in your early stages
Youve got to have a lot more lovers and a lot more rages.
But I cant spoil your fun
```

```
We dont have to take it
Never did + never will
Dont want no religion
And as far as we can tell
Were not gonna take it
From you or anyone
Were not gonna take you
Gonna stake you
Gonna rape you
Lets forget you
Better still
```

```
Hey Bobby lets both walk back together
Theres something important I have to tell yer
You know that deaf kid who lives next door
Well theres some strange goin's on and
                                    what is more
Whenever I see him standing in the garden,
I feel sort of dizzy and my muscles harden
And he seems to know whenever I'm watchin,
He smiles out to space I can feel him touching
me

Why dont you and me investigate
We dont have to be in bed 'till eight
Ill ask his mother if its all o.k.
For us to take him out to play
And then you'll see exactly what I mean
The way he lives an incredible dream
And somehow I feel he knows more than me
Despite that he cant hear or see

Hello Missus I've come to see Tommy
Brought him this present and this is Bobby
Can we go up and sit by his bed
Maybe he'll come to our garden instead

MOTHER:
Oh really Jim thats a wonderful thought
Both of you're welcome—Tom's on the porch
Just go out and touch him—he'll know that its you
If you need me I'll be in the front room

spoken: Thanks Missus!
        Come on Bobby!!
```

A selection of Pete Townshends lyrics from the time when "Tommy" was still at the ideas stage, before the album, the opera and the film.

The whole focal point of Tommy, the real beginning was "The Amazing Journey". Here is the story as it stood at that time before we began recording :-

> I awoke on Tuesday morning
> My illness much improved
> In fact I felt fantastic,
> My spirits ache removed.
> And so I tried to move again,
> At first it was a strain,
> And so I fell back on my bed,
> My head and heart in pain.
>
> At twelve my mum brought dinner,
> At four my mum brought tea,
> At eight my mum brought supper
> And ten o'clock brought sleep
> And sleep brought moods and yearning
> To travel just once more,
> That one amazing journey
> I slept through once before.
>
> Sickness will surely take the mind
> Where minds can't usually go
> Come on the amazing journey
> And learn all you should know.
>
> A vague haze of delirium creeps up on me.

> Then at once a tall stranger I suddenly see
> He's dressed in a silver sparked glittering gown
> And his golden beard flows nearly down to the ground
> His eyes are the eyes that transmit all they know
> And sparkle warm crystalline glances to show
> That he is your leader and he is your guide,
> On the amazing journey together you'll ride.
>
> The dream that I'm dreaming is a vision it seems
> For now reality itself appears in dreams
> I know that here's my Master, my guide and saviour.
>
> The face so young, the hands so clean, the eyes so bright
> And the build so lean, as though the man has lived just today,
> But the wisdom is clear and so is the way.
> My bedroom fades as I fall through my life,
> The illness is gone and my Master's ahead, calling me on.
> We walk through the city, the streets I know well,
> Until we arrive at a place I don't know,
> The grass seems to relish our toes and our heels,
> And the flowers the wind and the pollen the bees
> Fishes lay writhing in shrinking puddles of silver.
> The tall trees, golden leafed, joined hands overhead
> Making a shadowed avenue. No shafts of sunlight
> But lines of nodding seekers, clothed in the robes
> Of their order. And pointing the way to us.
> They pointed within and my Master decided

That at least they were faced the right way
Even if rooted to the spot by preconceptions.
One spoke and said, "We one day will follow."
So we took off our shoes and set off through the hollow
Tunnel created by the sun seeking trees
And set off on our journey
Forever at peace.

Soon we spotted a pinpoint of light
Far off in the distance and just within sight.
The master decreed that the end was near
But this singing sensation was a sign.
As we drew nearer the first ray of light
A shock wave hit us and threw us apart

I am alone. More alone in my ignorance now than ever before.
At least before I thought I knew what life was about.
Despite the knowledge that I know this is a test
I'm petrified and clouds of worry and fear smelling
Like animal sweat and shivering, quaking besets me.
The darkness of this place is unbelievable.
It's so dark it clouds my mind. As though this
Is where nothing only exists. But fear.

And now an oasis, like rebirth, the rush of blood
And the straining, basic drive to see the light.
Trapped in womb-like darkness, my mind is
Creating its own lying illusion to save its sanity.
Here, my mother, here my father, here other
Reasons to cling to prejudged life as I know it.
Warmth and cool, food and love, belongings of
Immeasurable value pile up around me.
I value them myself.
Placing a label on each friend, article and emotion
That appears.

And then without warning I was back at my Master's side.
Immediately aware of the object of the first lesson
I had learnt that whatever situation my Master prescribed
I should accept without question. Not immediately reverting
To the illusory plan and skating on the ice of life's pleasure.
With guidance from my beloved Master, who seemed to
Know the overgrown path so well, we quickly found the
Shaft of light we had spotted earlier.

A little taller at his side I travelled on.
We travelled for what seemed like an eternity;
The Master never speaking or making any signs,
Just smiling occasionally and then bowing his head as we walked
As though concerned with things outside himself.
The things we saw were unparalleled in beauty.
Loaded with knowledge and meaning, each vision imparting a little
Of each. Awesome mountains, never so huge.
Yawning holes in the earth so deep that we had to wait
Four long years to hear a replying question to my shout.
I would have fallen asleep and missed the echo when it came
Had not the Master awakened me in the nick of time.
He knew when it was due. He seemed to know every inch of the way.
Pointing out every wonderful sight, intense chemical colours
Bubbling in molten metal ; incredible rippling hues in
The spray of the waterfalls as the fine sunlight struck them ;
Birds of the air and other animals that I'd never seen before
So ancient, so new, ranging between indescribable beauty
And indescribable ugliness. Everything was being absorbed.
Sometimes, though, the Master would halt. Looking at me harshly
He would send my contented and happy soul to a spot
Way, way, back on our path. I would have to retrace all my steps
To find him once more. Sometimes the awesome beauty of
Many of the wonders on the way would hold me up.
He would always be patiently waiting when I finally arrived at his side
Not speaking a forgiving word, but reminding me
By his very existence that I am forgiven.

Chart showing Creation, Evolution, Reincarnation, Involution

I am lost. An eternity must have passed since I felt enlightenment.
Eons must have passed since I made any progress towards my Lord.
I am perpetually praying to him for guidance, but he never answers.
I am beginning to believe that he has carried on without me.
One life is all I know. The present life.
And yet because of my ignorance of the infinite
I cannot enjoy it. I am sad, poor, wrapped in indignity
And not aware of any of the knowledge I may have
Stumbled upon in the past. Is there a past/ a future ?
Is there an eternity ? My pathetic cry for reward falls on hardened ears.
As time passes boredom forces me to amuse myself.
I marry and justify a lifetime of obsessed moneymaking
In order to keep my family. I justify an eternity of oblivious
Dreaming to counter the strain of all my money making.

And again, like a flash I see the vision of my Master.
Ever patient. Totally forgiving. All knowing, waiting
At the exact spot I left him. I quickly run towards him,
Bringing my wife and family, bringing my business partners
And odd acquaintances who had shown interest in my Amazing Journey.
I know the ground so well, and we hurry along, occasionally
Waiting while some of our party absorb an amazing sight.
There is no real rush, we are again aware of eternity.

Soon I was back at my Masters side, even taller.
I now had company on my amazing journey,
Apart from my Master, all those in my heart,
Funny how they all learnt from what I had been through,
How easy it was my love to impart.
The Master looked fondly at my wife and our children,

and Realization, according to Meher Baba. (see key, below right)

Or even what to look for. I had to find the answer myself.

So here I am again. Completely in the dark.
Reading every book I can lay my hands on,
Listening to every Tom, Dick, or Harry who can offer an answer,
Or even a question. Complete confusion reigns in my mind
And once more my heart sinks into the mire of life.
When the wind blows, I am chilled, even though I am the wind.
When the midday sun shines, I sweat, even though I am the sun.
When the stars twinkle in the heavens I wonder how, though I know.
Tossed like a paper plane in the wind, like a cork in a storm,
I look for answers. Occasionally I grasp some minor detail
Of evolution which helps me on my way. And so encouraged I
Lecture my children, telling them how wise I am in my experience.
And they in turn, laugh and tell me of things so new that
I bow in shame and reverence to them, aware only of my ignorance.

I await. A slave of evolutions infinite, unending drive towards . . . .
And so . . . .
Each time I questioned, I fell.
Eventually, numbed by nillness and negativity, I slept.
Though I was sleeping, the world still went round and round.
Mothers gave birth to children and Undertakers collected the dead.
And as I lay oblivious for millions of years, men killed men,
And laughed at their victims, learning nothing.
And then receiving forgiveness, forgot that forgiveness
And remembered only that which they'd been forgiven.
They died, only to be followed by men with more hate
And more lust. Men abused men and were perpetually re-incarnated
Until they learned to love their brothers. Indeed,
To learn that other men were their brothers, not their slaves
Or enemies. Life after life they would experience until
They could only forgive. And when they kissed, thought only
Of that kiss, and not of the pleasures of the seduction,
Or the deceit of their love for another. When they gave gifts
Thought only of the giving and not of the reasons for giving,
Or of what might be gained by giving.
Giving without having to justify giving.
Taking without having to justify taking.
Loving without having to justify loving.

All this went on. As one man attained these merits,
Another man was conceived without them, as one child was born divine,
Another was born mortal.
As one man found within himself the truth, another began to look.

And so it went on.
As it was when he first began to sleep,
It was when he awoke. And when I awoke it was by my Masters side.

I was delighted and warmly greeted him and caressed him as though
We had not seen each other for years, but the Master
Acted as though I had never been away. As though I hadn't been
Through countless reincarnations since I first slept.
I knew yet another truth.

His eyes informing them that his will was theirs.
And I for my part spent every hour with the family
Waiting until they were ready to start.

But soon came the time when no more help was in me,
To teach them all more I had to learn more myself.
And so with the Master I set off once more
And nearer myself and my goal I headed forth.
The path this time was rough and uphill,
I often took rest while my Master stood still
And wondered how he, no stronger than I, could manage
To climb without fatigue and decline.
The mountain grew steeper and the crags sharply bent
The crevices full of fresh snow and ice, crystals reflected the sun,
So brilliantly that I nearly lost my balance several times.
Each time the thoughts of the Master would enter my mind,
And the very knowledge of his presence would save me.
Up, up, in search of the summit we climbed.
Each time a new height was attained a new one became apparent.
Then one morning as the sun's mellow warmth awoke me
I realized my position. Here was the tallest mountain in
The whole of the universe, and yet when I climbed it
What did I find? Only myself. If I had climbed a mountain
Any higher I would still only find myself. Maybe if I
Searched every jungle in the cosmos I would find the throne of the LORD.
Perhaps if I ransacked the Ocean floors on every planet
In every galaxy, in every universe in the infinite cosmos
I would find him. The Master gravely shook his head and I
Knew that despite his infinite wisdom, infinite power, infinite awareness
That he would not, could not tell me where to look.

This chart (left), painted by Rano Gayley under the supervision of Meher Baba, is a pictorial version of the book **God Speaks.**

God in the Beyond Beyond State represents God as pure Essence, infinite, original and eternal, unaware of anything, even of Himself. God Is.

God in the Beyond State represents the Oversoul (Paramatma), essentially the same as God in the Beyond Beyond State except that here surged the whim to know Himself and He became conscious of infinite power, knowledge and bliss; and simultaneously conscious of Illusion which manifested as the Creation. By completing His journey through the worlds of forms He sheds the illusion of their apparent reality.

Reading counter-clockwise, the first forms taken by souls emanating from the Creation point are gaseous. As consciousness evolves, souls take the innumerable forms indicated, experiencing increasing impressions (sanskaras). Arriving at the state of man, the soul has achieved complete consciousness and reincarnates innumerable times until it is ready to experience involution, all of which takes place while embodied in the gross world.

While getting free of sanskaras, the ascending soul gradually becomes aware of the seven planes and higher spheres until it is liberated from all bindings and becomes one with God (God-realized).

The first three planes depict subtle awareness; the fourth portrays the vast powers and energies encountered there; the fifth is the plane of sainthood and is in the mental sphere; the sixth is the plane of illumination and the seventh is the plane of God-realization, i.e. unity with God.

> I longed for the day when my Master and I could be as one,
> That very longing threw me back, but this time not far.
> I had learned so much from all, the experiences I had known
> That I too, was gaining some of the power of my Master to control myself.
> We journeyed on again, this time, quite simply, the Master
> Showed me the wonders of my own mind. Everything I imagined became
> Reality and all I had experienced was laid out before me
> In order that I could recap and benefit from all I knew and thought.
> When I had gazed in awe at all I already knew the Master
> Showed me the creatures from all over the cosmos.
> Each one more confounding than the next, but all with the same aim.
> Each one amazed me and many were completely beyond
> Anything I had ever imagined. Many existed on planes and spheres
> Beyond my imagination. Many lived in terms of existence that
> Defied explanation, many had to be viewed through the body of
> One of their kind in order to utilise their radically different senses.
> And see them at all.

The story is poetry, sometimes good, often terrible. It was all stream of consciousness stuff, but when I read it back then, it staggered me. I realised that I had described a story that I could never have dreamed of myself let alone put to music.

But the strangest part of all is that there was no development stage between this Hesse-like tale of mystery and spiritual intrigue, and what we today see to be Tommy. I just lived with the story, invented a name for my hero, Tommy, and started to write songs. I got Tommy's name from mid-air, but it suited. The middle letters were OM which was aptly mystical, and it was an English name associated with the war and heroism. It was also fairly close to To-Me, again you can see the obvious spiritual bent.

Tommy became deaf, dumb and blind when I realised that there was no way to get across, musically or dramatically, the idea of our ignorance of reality, as I had learned it to be, from reading Meher Baba.

Meher Baba talked of our lives being led in an 'illusion'; that we were dreaming; that reality was Infinite, and that we would realise that Infinity only through denying the lust, greed and anger of the material world, through love, and starting our journey "back" to God.

I realised that there was a parallel in the shape of the autistic child. Strangely enough, I have now come across the treatment of Professor Nordoff who managed to bring autistic children out of their 'dream' through a combination of love and music.

This was a straightforward analogy because the word 'illusion' is used by Meher Baba in a mystical sense. In other words the illusion that we live in, is one where our senses are fully functioning – we have our five senses and we have our emotions, and so on and so forth, but there are whole chunks of life, including the whole concept of reality, which escapes us. We don't really know who we are, we don't really know how we got here, and we don't really know what our aim is, we don't understand the concept of infinity, and our mi s are unable to accept it. We don't understand suffering or what causes it, we don't understand life itself or what motivates it, we can't accept death and we feel it to be unjust (although it is part of the wheel of life). So I decided that the hero had to be deaf, dumb and blind, so that, seen from our already limited point of view, his limitations would be symbolic of our own.

With a background like this, even The Who could not disguise the heavy mystical qualities of the story of Tommy. Even though the original plan was eventually lost and the story made more real and organic, the music more contemporary and reachable than the dreary stuff I had recorded on demos, there was still a strong thread of spirituality. Our record producer Kit Lambert said that he had to remain detached from the theme's aims in order to be objective. I think he warmed far more to the idea of 'Rock Opera' than 'God Opera.' Still, while we were pottering about in the studio at IBC trying to pull an unfinished story into shape, while I was rewriting lyrics to songs about other things to make them fit, while John was busy at home dealing with a 'commission' from me to 'write something horrible', while all this was going on, Tommy was carrying on where the above story left off.

The malleability of the story of Tommy, the fact that it

Two people who were closely involved with the Who's Tommy album: Kit Lambert (right) who produced the original album, and Mike McInnerney (below) who conceived and painted the album cover (bottom of page).

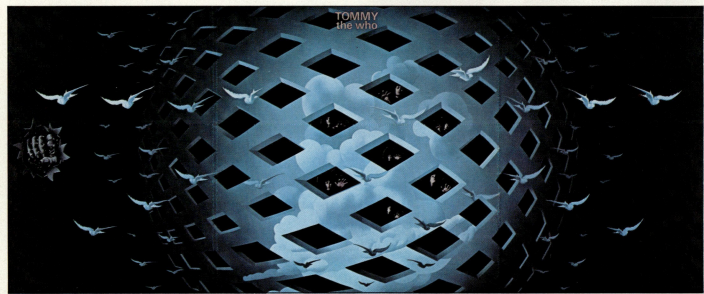

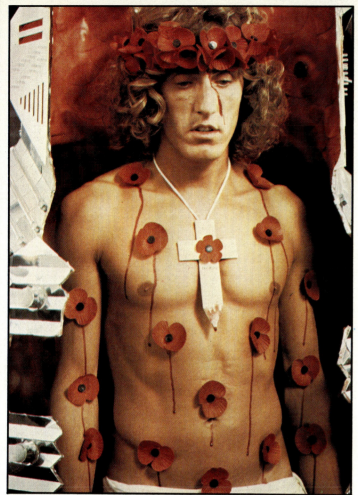

(Above) The religious nature of Russell shows itself.
(Below) Peter Townshend works closely with dubbing editor Terry Rawlings (left) and editor Stuart Baird (centre).

seemed to stand up, even in a highly edited or abridged form, allowed The Who to select only material suited to the simple line of the group, to be featured live on stage. I will never forget that tour, the finale of Tommy never failed to mesmerise me along with the audience. It always felt to me like a prayer, I always felt myself full of Meher Baba when we performed it.

Our managers' skill at promotion and exploitation turned Tommy into a world-respected work. We performed it at opera houses all round the world.

In Germany we are, to this day, excused local taxes because we are considered to be a 'cultural' event. In New York we were the first group to play at the Met., and later Woodstock brought Tommy into the charts again and to its second life.

Its third life came when it was 'symphonised' by Lou Reisner. Lou had some arrangers put the score across in a fully orchestral way, using traditional techniques. The original Who version was adhered to as a basis, although every part was played by a different notable Rock singer or personality. I was charmed by the record Lou Reisner made, as it brought to life the whole original idea I had for "Rael". At last I was to hear something I had written, played by a grand orchestra. Later on, particularly after being involved in live performances of this version I grew disenchanted with it. It seemed bleak, even though it had much that the original never had and brought Tommy to a whole new audience.

One of the new audience was Ken Russell, who admitted to me that he preferred the orchestral version to the original group version. I think he grew to change his mind, but it goes to show how Tommy's long and varied history has affected an expanding audience.

When I first came to meet Ken Russell he lived up to his reputation. He was describing a film he was forced to abort, about the Rabelasian monks. Hairy stuff I can tell you. Chris Stamp, one of our managers, and myself, listened quietly, and wondered if he was really the right man for the job. We had been totally convinced up to that point.

I felt convinced, more through a coincidence than anything else. I'm a great believer that coincidence is an indication of higher forces at work, although I'll be first to admit it's a small world and all that. On the day I met Ken Russell I was strolling around London recording street noises in stereo for the "Quadrophenia" album. I had my tape machine in a suitcase and the mikes concealed in a holdall.

At the time I was after 'casual conversation'. I saw an interesting group and sidled sideways up to them pointing my holdall into their midst. The conversation I heard was fascinating. In the group were Ken Russell, Chris Stamp and Mike Carrearas, who were all unhappy that they hadn't been able to locate me that afternoon for a meeting they were about to have. As you can imagine, I just felt all this meant that the film HAD TO BE.

Later meetings with Ken revealed a very spiritual man. He was deeply interested in the mystical thematic frame of Tommy, and I showed him, or talked to him about, all of the material discussed or revealed in this article. One thing that he seemed keen to do, however, and this was clearly a necessity, was to make the story work on an everyday level.

I had tried desperately during the recording of Tommy to make the story work. When Tommy walked out of one door I wanted everyone to feel he walked into another in the next song. In the end though, Tommy was disjointed and took quite a lot of explaining. The death sequence, for example, where Tommy's father kills his mother's new suitor, had no 'moment of death'. I had originally intended this to be added on the surface some amazing heart-shaking sound that would let you know the terrible deed had been done – before the parents launched into, "You Didn't Hear It, You Didn't See It!" On the original Tommy album, it is easy to forgive those who listening, asked, "Didn't see what?". In the film, Ken Russell redesigned the whole sequence. The Mother's lover kills the father, the father then becomes an allegory for the 'Master' I talked of in my early notes. The vision of Tommy's father serves as the symbol of his spiritual focus. Even so, quite a few people, after seeing the film, asked me, "What did they do with the body?"

As you can see (right) Ken, in the first few pages of his script, had introduced a lot of visual material, a lot of action that did not have suitable music. Later in his second draft script he introduced a number of other places where new action was brought in to strengthen up the story line. One song in particular I remember writing was called "Deceived".

I based this rather long song on the chords of "I'm Free" as I didn't want too many new musical themes brought in. I felt Tommy already had a few too many. "Deceived" was a song set towards the pinnacle of Tommy's success as a spiritual leader. He cried out to the world through loud speakers on the streets, and via the media, that war, politics, religion, all were useless for those who were searching for truth. "Deceived" was a powerful song that was excluded eventually from the script. It ended up much abridged as "TV Studio".

I'M FREE – I'M FREE
Turn your backs on wars there's peace ahead
I'M FREE – I'M FREE
Time for change, forget the pointless deaths
TO ME – COME TO ME
Walk beside me free of wordly fears
WITH ME – BE WITH ME
Leave behind false promises and tears
SENSATION – I'M A SENSATION
SENSATION – I'M A SENSATION
And I'm waiting for you to follow me
DECEIVED – ALL DECEIVED
As silence reigns the stocks and shares still rise
REPRIEVE – AT LAST REPRIEVE
They capitalize on every tear and sigh
I'M FREE – I'M FREE
Truth to hear and speak and truth to see
I'M FREE – I'M FREE
Forget them all, the way is clear to see
I'M FREE – I'M FREE
I'm waiting for you to follow me
DECEIVED – ALL DECEIVED
The hypocrites and war lords turn to craw
REPRIEVE – AT LAST REPRIEVE
The wars you fight in only pay for more
SENSATION – I'M A SENSATION
SENSATION – I'M A SENSATION
And I'm waiting for you to follow me
BE FREE – COME TO ME
The men you mourn all stand among you now
BE FREE – BE WITH ME
They dance around the stone to which you bow
I'M FREE – I'M FREE
Forget them all the way is clear to see
I'M FREE – I'M FREE
Don't waste every lifetime looking back
SENSATION – I'M A SENSATION
SENSATION – I'M A SENSATION
And I'm waiting for you to follow me
Good morning converts
That was your new Messiah
Calling out for you to come and follow him
So jump on the buses
Never mind the fares
Off you go to Tommy's
The answer to your prayers

"Champagne" was another song Ken wanted me to write, this time the song was included in the film. Ken felt that people would want to feel Tommy's mother was a real person. What had wealth done to her now that her son was a famous pinball champ? In fact "Champagne" turns out to be a heavy Ken Russell statement (overstatement?)

TOMMY

As the giant sun sinks below the horizon the camera pans with it to CAPTAIN & MRS WALKER lying side by side on a mountain top. They have just made love. With linked hands they walk down the mountainside in the gathering twilight. They kiss in a glade near a waterfall and drink of its sparkling water. Darkness falls as they walk off through the wood – metallic paper strips (anti-radar devices) fall softly around them like diamond snowflakes.

As they come through the trees into the open we see a balloon barrage floating on the night air like a captive cloud. Ack Ack shells burst in the sky like white lightning.

The COUPLE hurry through burning, deserted streets towards the station as unseen planes drone overhead. Searchlights try to sweep them from the sky. In an orange glow the FIREMAN stokes his boiler. The LOVERS hurry past the engine and have barely reached the first carriage before the GUARD blows his whistle. Doors slam. A quick tearful kiss, clasped hands breaking apart as the train moves off. CAPTAIN WALKER disappears into the darkness, waving, waving. MRS. WALKER waves too. She cries as she looks into the empty, black night.

CAPTAIN WALKER'S Wellington revs up on the tarmac. He clambers in. Chocks away. Soon the climbing plane is merely a silhouetted dragonfly against the moon. MRS. WALKER at home looks out of her window through a web of criss-crossed paper at the moon. The room is dark and she too is in silhouette.

CAPTAIN WALKER in his Wellington is surrounded by a kaleidoscope of bursting star shells and flak. His face shows not fear but a strange, heightened awareness of the beauty exploding around him.

In her darkened bedroom MRS WALKER stands before her dressing table mirror, staring with dreamy fondness at a large framed photo of Captain Walker's handsome smiling face. She picks it up, kisses it, holds it by the side of her own face and looks in the mirror at the happy couple. CRACK! – the mirror mysteriously fractures right across the middle of Captain Walker's face.

CRACK! An explosion just outside the cockpit sends CAPTAIN WALKER's plane spiralling hopelessly out of control.

MRS WALKER works on the assembly line at a munitions factory. Empty shell cases approach her in slow procession. She fills each one with a handful of highly polished ball bearings. Music while you work. An OFFICIAL, accompanied by the FLOOR MANAGER, comes up to MRS WALKER and hands her a telegram. She hesitates, senses what it contains, then opens it quickly – a prolonged pause then collapse to the floor and a flailing hand grasping a box for support. As it overturns silver balls cascade and run all around her.

Fanfares etc: celebration from "Its A Boy"

Colourful bunting, Union Jacks, flags and streamers. VE day. The camera pulls back to reveal a hospital delivery room. MRS WALKER sweats in labour. A son is born. Great jubilation and cheering – not for TOMMY (or is it?) but for the General driving by in a car outside – part of the victory parade.

MRS WALKER holds TOMMY in her arms. By the side of the bed a bunch of flowers. The camera moves towards them. The petals drop off – only the skeleton stalks remain. Dissolve through to a single poppy.

Possible shadowing melody between "Booms"

Remembrance Day. The poppy is on a small wooden cross in MRS WALKER's hand. Guns boom. By her side TOMMY stands to attention. The guns are quiet. The 2 minutes silence is over. MRS WALKER plants her cross among a thousand similar crosses and kisses TOMMY. Zoom into crosses and ranks of artificial red poppies. Red fills the screen.

Tommy's holiday camp – new words – seduction

Red fills the screen. The camera pulls back to show a red-jacketed holiday camp host. He shakes hands with MRS WALKER, pats TOMMY on the head. The TWO GROWNUPS look at each other and are attracted to each other. He carries her suitcases to a chalet. TOMMY follows behind.

Mother should say something

LATER. MRS WALKER & the REDCOAT are smooching together at the camp dance. TOMMY sits by himself sucking an orangeade through a straw. Later all three of them leave the camp. Now they are home. MRS WALKER tucks TOMMY in. The REDCOAT, having discarded his jacket, lurks discreetly outside the door. On TOMMY's bedside table is the portrait we saw earlier of CAPTAIN WALKER. Next to it is a model of his Wellington bomber. MOTHER kisses TOMMY good night and goes out. TOMMY looks at his father's photograph then closes his eyes. The room grows darker. CAPTAIN WALKER smiles at TOMMY from his photo frame.

A bar of light appears beneath the door. The door opens. The figure of a MAN stands silhouetted in the doorway. He walks towards the bed. It is CAPTAIN WALKER. Softly, gently, he touches the head of his sleeping son, tiptoes back to the door and turns for a last look at TOMMY, who wakes up to see the silhouette a split second before it closes the door.

OVERTURE TO BE REWRITTEN after filming

The early part of the script which needed extra music and sound effects from Townshend. The love scene (above) and the blitz scene (below) both had musical backing. (left) A time-sheet for the champagne sequence. Townshend had to invent a sound effect resembling chocolate hitting a picture.

on decadence in contemporary society. A brilliant scene in the film I think, the music for this song was again inspired by "I'm Free" of the original version. In fact, the only other song written specially for the film. "Bernie's Holiday Camp" took as its base the "Tommy's Holiday Camp" of the original.

Ken's real contribution to the evolution of Tommy came with his visual reaction to many of the stories' surface events. The "Acid Queen" he saw as a superb opportunity to put across the seedy glamour of the hooker/pusher with real venom. In "Champagne", the musical demands made on myself can be easily appreciated by glancing at the timing sheet I was presented with, when the number was extended to include a bit of extra decadence. (above)

Writing the new material for Tommy was a pleasure in fact, I felt several years later, detached from Tommy. The Who as a group only played a short section of it on the stage, and most of the new music and incidental music came easily. But for me, the real Tommy still lies in three or four songs, a few pieces of paper and the mystery that only a writer can ever understand. The mystery of writing something that takes on a life of its own and leaves you far, far behind still trying to discover how to turn the dreamlike events of Tommy's life into fact. Ken Russell's film reveals that it was a dream, that it could never, as we had eventually got it down onto record, ever happen in reality. In my head it happened, and maybe one day . . . maybe one day nothing.

SO YOU record the world's first rock opera, and the critics go wild, and it sells like hot pintables, and your band gets more and more famous, and everyone loves you and the film offers come flooding in and the next year you've got a box-office super-smash in the movies as well. Right? No ladies and gentlemen, when the film business and the music business push their heads together you get something like a dinosaur. Dinosaurs move slowly.

Of course, to make a film of 'Tommy' was a natural development. As the years went by it was subjected to various interpretations, from ballet to school end-of-term entertainment, but somehow the film didn't get made.

Pete Townshend: "I suppose one thing that slowed us down was that initially we were very ambitious for it. It was an ambitious recording project, and when it was finished we got such good critical acclaim from the British Press we naturally thought it would be easy to set up the sort of film we wanted because it was such hot property. But the film industry at the time was very belligerent, and still is in its old frame of mind, and there were contractual loopholes. We had to offer it first to Universal, who were tied up with our record company in America, MCA, and this is where the first hold-up came. They agreed to finance it and distribute it and Kit Lambert (manager) was appointed to draft the screenplay, which actually turned out to be very similar to the one Ken has done now. Universal hated the screenplay, but they took two years to say so, and by that time I was getting very frustrated".

There was a three-sided row going between Pete, Universal and Kit Lambert. Universal hated Lambert's screenplay, and there was no way they'd put up the money for his film of 'Tommy'. Pete was frustrated and blaming Lambert for the film not getting made. "Our relationship never really recovered", he says. "I saw it very much in black and white at the time". The two-year delay had somewhat dampened the project's hot properties, and although the 'Woodstock' film revived interest in it, as did the Lou Reisner orchestral production, still they couldn't find the right man to make it. Ken Russell was approached, and said he'd like to do it, maybe in 1975 because of his other plans. That didn't help feelings of frustration and impatience either. They met other potential directors: "They would insist", says Townshend, "on buying me long drawn-out lunches 'to find out where your head is at' and to ask me how I felt about it because they wanted to 'fit in with your ideas and conception'. In the end I thought if they wanted me to come up with the ideas then they could give me the money and I'd make it". But the film industry doesn't chance its investments on guitarists and writers, even if they do have good ideas. And anyway, as Townshend has explained (see his interview) he was just as eager for someone else to take 'Tommy' and give it their works. Chapter two rather than a filmed re-make.

Someone like Ken Russell? In the end, Russell was the man—probably the best man,

PART TWO/FILMING TOMMY

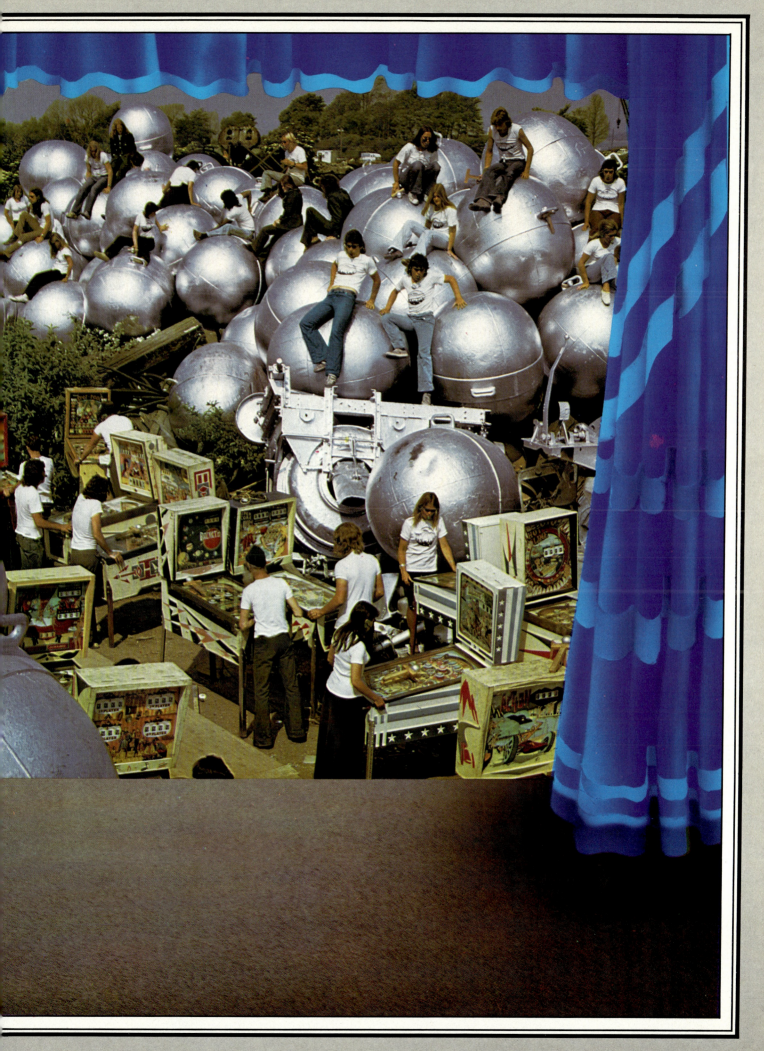

and possibly the only man to make the film. Robert Stigwood took the role of something like the fairy godfather who helped the dream come true. He got the deal together, negotiated the money, set up the deal with Columbia, got Russell together with the Who again, put in a lot of his own money, and accepted the traditional responsibility for casting. Townshend had his own ideas about casting (again see his interview) but Stigwood insisted on some good box-office pullers—like Ann-Margret, Jack Nicholson and Oliver Reed. In the event, Townshend came round to his point of view and admits that those people, to whom he objected in the early stages, work well in the film. It must have been a struggle though: "Robert Stigwood rang up and said he'd got Jack Nicholson, and I said 'Who's Jack Nicholson?' and he said he was one of the biggest stars in America at the moment. So I said 'Can he sing?' and he said no". Townshend's reaction was: "I'm not having another fucker in this film who can't sing. Oliver Reed's giving me nightmares as it is". It turned out that he could sing, and that Reed's style fitted the part. Such is the stuff of movie legend.

The mechanics of setting up a project like 'Tommy' are approximately this: the money is raised—quite how is shrouded in myth and mystery, but somehow it's there, at least on paper. The machine then grinds into action from the production office. The director is decided, and he gets a working script done, if it isn't already there: in this case Russell wrote his own. Then he starts assembling the crew—both the technicians and the actors—well in advance of shooting. Apart from the stars, the key members of the team are the executive producer, art director and assistant, lighting camera man, costume designer, props man, locations manager, set designer, and (in this case) musical director and choreographer. And the accountant—most important. Working in the film industry is a specialised branch of accountancy, and on 'Tommy' the man was Bobby Blues. The director comes with the shooting script, and the accountant goes through it, costing each scene. He'll then say 'you've got this amount of money so you either have to cut this, this and this or get more money'. Russell is reputed to have vowed to make his film his way if he had to raid every one of Robert Stigwood's piggy banks to do it. Ultimately, the money is the producer's responsibility.

We are still a long way from starting to shoot the film: the locations manager goes out looking for suitable places, bearing in mind not only their suitability for the camera, but whether they're near decent hotels, whether they can get extras easily, whether the catering van can get up to the set and a million other details including whether there's a pub nearby: film crews don't appreciate being kept dry. The props department goes into action, buying up anything from correct-period furniture to fake palm trees. The art director, his assistant, and the set designer get working on the sets and specially designed equipment, the costumes have to be designed and made, and the shooting schedule is drawn up. Accountant, producer and director are heavily involved in all this.

It had been decided early on that there would be no dialogue, that the soundtrack to the film would be entirely music, so simultaneously Townshend was in the Who's Ramport Studios getting it recorded. Russell's script called for two new songs and a great deal of re-writing of the original 'Tommy' material. The songs had to fit with Russell's projected timings for each sequence and the words had to explain what was happening—often in a much more literal way than the original had done. Yet both had to be flexible enough to expand or contract to ideas that might occur to Russell while he was filming, or in case some things didn't work out as planned. As it turned out, the music needed every ounce of flex it could muster.

The Who put down much of the basic music, with the actors singing their lead parts (with the exception of Young Tommy, Barry Winch, whose part is sung by Alison Dowling). But there was a host of guest musicians involved in the sessions: Elton John brought his whole entourage—band and Gus Dudgeon, his producer—to record his version of 'Pinball Wizard', and among the others on the sessions were Ronnie Wood and Kenny Jones of the Faces, Philip Chen, Alan Ross, Tony Newman, Caleb Quaye, Nicky Hopkins (who did most of the piano work), Jess Roden, Mick Ralphs of Bad Company,

Russell used 40 members of a group of hell's angels – the Black Angels from Sunderland – in the sequence for 'Sensation.' He was totally amazed when they began the fight. This was not the usual staged fight between stunt men, but a real no-holds-barred punch-up. They kicked and punched each other using bike chains as weapons. Although some were badly cut, Russell got them to do the whole sequence three times. They referred to the number of 'takes' he does, when they made him an honorary member of their group. The leather jacket they gave him had the words "One Last Time" printed in studs across the back. (Far left) Setting up to shoot the angels' camp-site. (Top) The fight starts. (Left) Waiting with a boot in the throat for a lens adjustment. (Right) They stop fighting and start dancing when they feel the effect of Tommy's powerful 'strange new vibrations' as he flies overhead on a hand-glider.

Chris Stainton, Mike Kellie, Fuzzy Samuels, Graham Deakin of John Entwistle's band Ox, Mylon LeFevre, Paul Gurvitz, Vicki Brown, Liza Strike and Margo Newman. Townshend brought in people with particular talents for specific parts: for instance Jess Roden came in to do a wailing, soulful voice part behind Roger Daltrey's lead on 'Listening To You'.

A lot of the backing vocals were done by Townshend and Billy Nichols, who worked continuously in Ramport for three weeks. They'd experiment for hours with different voice effects, always towards a specific complement to part of the scripted idea. Billy Nichols recalls being surprised at Russell's demeanor in the studio—he came to the sessions more often than not—which was far from the overbearing ego-mania the man's public reputation had led him to expect. There was even one piece Townshend had done on synthesiser which Russell said he could not use for the film because he wouldn't be able to match it visually.

"Towards the end of the sessions," Nichols says, "he seemed to get a little bit crazy. As the music was getting finished he would be walking around the studio with a stick in his hand, beating out rhythms, getting more excited, suggesting more ideas, maybe getting a bit more pissed than he would have done earlier on. You could see he was beginning to feel things happening, beginning to see what he'd be doing with the music".

Nichols also pointed up the difference between the musicians who came in to record, and the actors who were relatively new to recording studios.

When Paul Nicholas came in to do his Cousin Kevin song, he completely changed, completely assumed his acting as well as singing role as soon as he was in front of the microphone. "He became a different person, he was so evil. I was watching and I felt like punching him, I thought 'you bastard' . . . and then he came out and said 'was that all right then'? Changed back again. He did it in a couple of takes".

He remembers just one time when Russell was really taking an active role, directing the way the music should go: mostly he left it to Pete, but at the end of "We're Not Going To Take It" there had to be a kind of angry crowd backing voice track, slowly building up resentment and anger to the point where the kids rebel against Tommy and his set-up. It took them all one night and another session to get it down, and Russell stood behind the mike, urging them on and getting them at it.

In many ways, those sessions at Ramport laid the foundations for the film as importantly as Russell's script: Russell was obviously drawing inspiration from them, and Oliver Reed says Townshend's reaction to his voice gave him the idea of playing Frank as a kind of burlesque. But if Townshend found Reed funny in that strange situation, the actors like Reed must have found the situation equally odd. "I met Ken in an Italian restaurant", he said, "and for once I didn't have to pay the bill, and we went to the studio and there was this huge pint pot of brandy which concealed most of Pete Townshend who sounded like a cement grinder because he eats potato crisps all the time and Ken was filling his face with currants, nuts rather, and I sang a few notes and Pete fell about . . ." Ah, rock and roll—the poor man must have wondered what he'd let himself in for. He rose, of course, to the occasion and by the time the film was finished he proved himself the equal even of Keith Moon.

While all this was going on, shooting had not even started. But the team was gathering —carpenters, electricians, make-up people, the camera crew, assistant director, caterers, continuity girl, lights people, technicians and labourers or all kinds. For 'Tommy', the total crew was 88. The film business is almost completely freelance, with a crew coming together to make one picture, then splitting up and changing partners for the next like some vast amoebic mass. Russell likes to use people he knows and has worked with before, and quite a few of the 'Tommy' people went with him to make 'Liszt'—but by no means all.

The script was sorted out, the locations set, and the budget set at something around one million pounds for a shooting schedule of 12 weeks. It ended up costing around two million, with shooting extended to 22 weeks, with some special effects left to do. Mr. Stigwood can't have hidden his piggy banks very well.

You talk about
your woman
I wish you could see mine
You talk about
your woman
I wish you could see mine
Every time
she starts to love
She brings eyesight
to the blind
Oh yeah

You know her daddy
gave her magic
I can tell
by the way she walks
You know her daddy
gave her magic
I can tell
by the way she walks
Every time she starts to shake,
The dumb begin to talk
Talk, talk, talk!

She's got the power to heal you, never fear
Oh she's got the power to heal you, never fear
One word from her lips and the deaf can hear
Ohhhhhh Yeahhhh!

THE LOCATION they chose for Tommy's Holiday Camp—the Glade Of Contemplation to which Tommy's followers come to experience deafness, dumbness, blindness, pinball and the rampant consumerism of Frank and Uncle Ernie—was a scrapyard. Of course, being Ken Russell's film of 'Tommy', it wasn't just any scrapyard: This was Harry Pound's place on the sea-front at Portsmouth, and the scrap is mostly ex-services stuff—anything from old battleships and military tanks to buoys. The former pride of Britain's Senior Service gets its come-uppance here at Harry Pound's: it's used as props in a Ken Russell movie.

There are huge mounds of buoys painted silver—the props department had to scour Hampshire to get enough silver paint to turn them into outsize pinballs. There are rows of pinball machines that've have seen better days, all waiting an ignominious end as effects man Nobby Clarke and his team stuff them with paraffin-soaked carpet underfelt. The fire department stands by, slightly nervously. It would be no joke if Harry Pound's scrapyard was to catch alight. It's possibly one of the most awkward locations in the history of the cinema, and it's freezing cold.

In context of the 'Tommy' story, the scene is this: having achieved fame, fortune and near-Avatar status as the Pinball Wizard, the deaf, dumb and blind boy welcomes his followers to his holiday camp, where they are told they must share his experiences if they are truly to follow him. They have to pay to get in, they have to buy their Tommy t-shirts and their Tommy crosses . . . they begin to realise they're being conned. They turn on Tommy and his entourage with their battle hymn "We're Not Going To Take It". As the tide turns and the revolution gets heavy, Tommy finds his mother and step-father dead . . .

Oliver Reed and Ann-Margret are lying in the freezing cold, on the muddy ground of Harry Pound's junkyard. Ken Russell and his team are standing over them, trying to work out their best camera angles and shots. Someone suggests they move Ollie over a bit—so he's lying half in a puddle. Ollie's the complete professional, really earning his money: he and Ann-Margret even have a technique for stopping shivering (corpses don't shiver) when the cameras are running. But move him into a puddle? "Hey Ken", he says. "Let's make it an art film".

It's been a trying few days in the junkyard: the giant pinballs have to constantly be re-painted as people clambering all over them with muddy shoes keep taking the silver off: the weather hasn't been kind to the crew—blazing sunshine alternates with pouring rain, playing havoc with the continuity. The fight sequence has demanded stunt-men as Ollie Reed gets stabbed, and Ann-Margret has to be hit over the head with a bottle and kicked. Now Ann-Margret is expensive, and accident prone. Everyone is nervous that she might really get hurt, and in the end Ken Russell takes the plunge himself.

Two bottles made of sugar are brought up, so they only have two chances for this take. The director kicks over one and smashes it—everyone on the set breathes a huge sigh of relief. If anyone else had goofed like that he would have exploded. They get it in the one take—without accident to Ann-Margret. Russell also puts the boot in without damage. The show goes on.

Now that they've reached the uprising scenes, it's important that they carry on and finish, whatever the hardships: with the

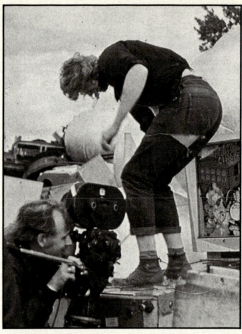

(Top left) Close-up shot of a pin-table being destroyed.
(Above) Ollie, lying in mud, jokes with Ann-Margret.
(Top right) Russell hits Ann-Margret with a bottle made of sugar and partly filled with red dye. As it smashes she is realistically splattered with blood. The dye used for blood is known as 'Kensington gore.' Russell paints on more 'gore' to bloody face (left and below right).
(Right) Roger Daltrey gets another boot in the face.
(Below left) One of the less comfortable things about being a film star. After hours of shivering in a muddy puddle, Ollie demanded, "Let's make this an art film Ken!"
(Far right) The camera precedes the line of revolting converts they march through Tommy's Holiday Camp, and destroy it. A more peaceful view of 'The Glade of Contemplation' as it called, is shown on pages 34 & 35

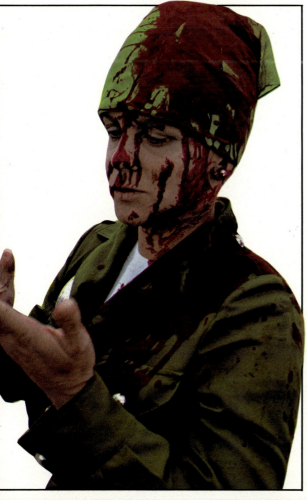

leading characters covered in mud and their clothes in rags, it would be virtually impossible to maintain accurate continuity the next day. So they press on. The next scene is where Tommy has to run for his life through a corridor of blazing pintables—a sprint through some 140 yards of flame. Most of it looks OK, the space is fairly wide, but there are sections where the gap between the tables is pretty narrow: the camera is on a track, it's covered in asbestos and the operators too have protective suits. Russell doesn't bother —he's too involved in what he's doing—and of course Roger Daltrey has no choice. Nobby Clarke demonstrates his flames, the firemen have given what seems to be a slightly reluctant OK, and Roger Daltrey seems to be finding it hard to believe he's got to run through *that*. He's really being put through the hoop on his debut film, doing things that a more hardened actor might well refuse to do. The hairdressers, make-up ladies and dressers have formed a kind of Save Our Roger society, and suck their teeth in righteous indignation: "Just look what that man's making our Roger do now."

He does it, running hard through the flaming corridor, and gets through. They take it. Right says Russell, we can get another take out of this. He does it again, they take it. Right says Russell, just once more. Daltrey does it again, he's exhausted: the third time a sudden burst of flame caught his hair and singed him a bit. With a sigh of relief that it was the final take, he falls back against a giant pinball, and springs away again. It was red-hot and burnt his arm. Daltrey and Russell walk away, knackered, from the set: from the assembled crew, a voice calls out "Ready when you are Ken".

He shouldn't have joked about it—he thought they'd finished for the day.

Among the crew, the production team of 'Tommy' weren't exactly noted for their generosity; they weren't given to handing out free booze or anything. So a kind of wry amusement mixed with grumbling hostility greeted the arrival of crates of whisky and brandy on the set that afternoon. A little sweetening was afoot for the extra overtime request—they wanted to shoot the final bit of that fire sequence, where Daltrey has to leap through yet more flames and past a tank. Of course they did it.

Perhaps that wasn't a typical day in the life of the 'Tommy' film, but neither was it that extreme. And it made a fine piece of film. Pete Townshend regards it as one of the movie's best sequences: "It seemed to bring the whole thing home to me. It gives the story a stark reality I had not realised, and I personally found it staggering and very moving."

Setting up some of the more elaborate scenes is an operation worthy of some of the Great Campaigns—for instance, the Pinball Wizard filming at the King's Theatre, Southsea, where Tommy beats the reigning Pinball Champ (Elton John). They rented the theatre by the day, but there was a show each evening which meant the crew had to work through the night dismantling the show scenery and erecting the Pinball Wizard set in time for filming to start at 7.30 in the morning. The set was built in sections and had never been fitted together before they had to do it for the first day's filming—a fact which irritated Terry Snow. "If they'd paid out £1,000 they could have had that theatre for a week day and night, and they wouldn't have had to pay out a fortune in overtime". It was a scramble to

The most dangerous thing Roger Daltrey had to do was to run through a 100 yard long corridor of blazing pin-tables. This was for the final part of the 'Tommy's Holiday Camp' scene. Tommy had just seen his mother and her lover killed and the camp totally destroyed. He stumbles through the burning camp singing, "See me, feel me." As it is a fairly close tracking shot, it had been decided that a stunt-man would not be used. The camera and crew were protected by asbestos sheeting (above). Russell was too involved and excited to get burned. The pin-tables (over 80 of them) had been carefully prepared by special-effects man Nobby Clark and his team. They were stuffed with paraffin-soaked rolls of carpet underfelt and fitted with concealed gas jets. Twenty firemen with hoses at the ready, and a water tender stood by. A previous fire on this particular site (a scrap yard) had taken days

to get under control and they were worried by the stunt. Originally only one take was thought possible but Russell got three. On the first, Roger singed his eyebrows and hair, and after the second he badly burned his arm when he rested against a giant pinball which had become red hot. He is holding his arm during his third run (right). Russell had some footage of the fire at Southsea pier edited into this scene at the end (see report pages 70 & 71).

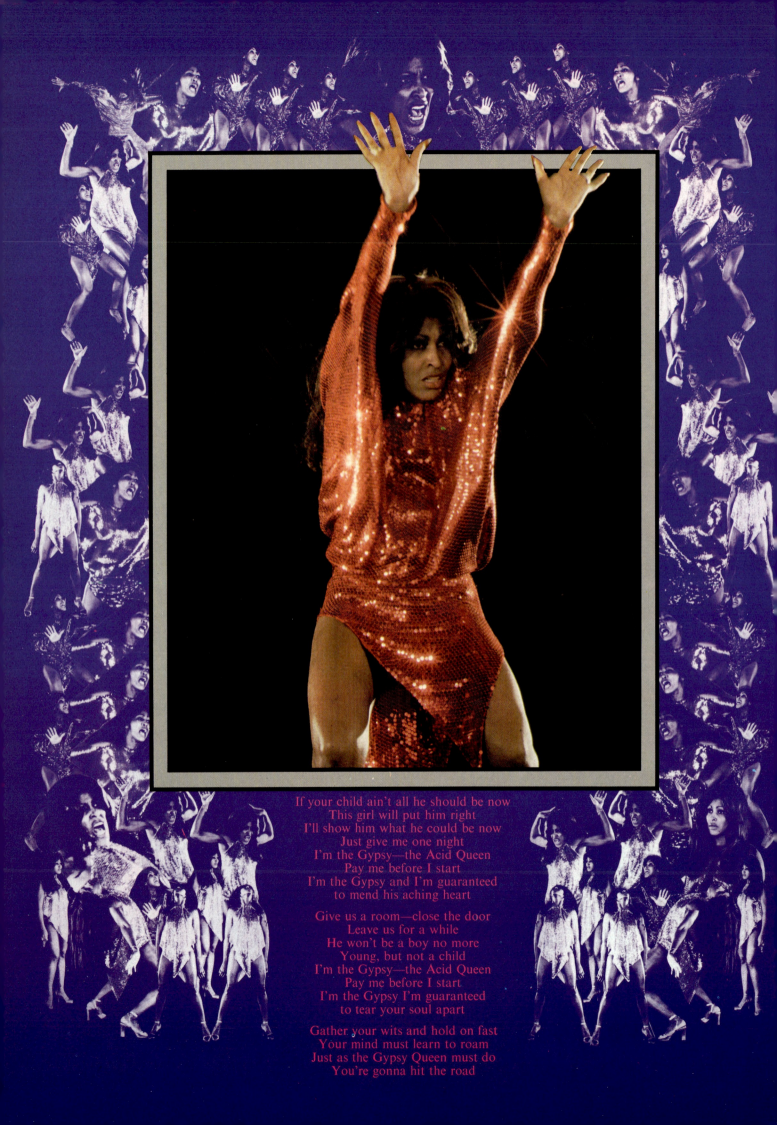

If your child ain't all he should be now
This girl will put him right
I'll show him what he could be now
Just give me one night
I'm the Gypsy—the Acid Queen
Pay me before I start
I'm the Gypsy and I'm guaranteed
to mend his aching heart

Give us a room—close the door
Leave us for a while
He won't be a boy no more
Young, but not a child
I'm the Gypsy—the Acid Queen
Pay me before I start
I'm the Gypsy I'm guaranteed
to tear your soul apart

Gather your wits and hold on fast
Your mind must learn to roam
Just as the Gypsy Queen must do
You're gonna hit the road

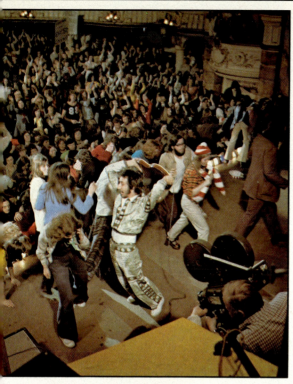

Pete Townshend couldn't get into 'prancing around on stage pretending to play with an unplugged guitar.' So the Who had several tons of amplifiers set up and played live for filming the 'Pinball Wizard' sequence.
When Keith Moon starts destroying his drum kit and Pete starts smashing his guitar (below left and right) the crowd react like the true professionals they weren't. About two hundred storm the stage helping to make it one of the film's most exciting scenes.
Unfortunately a girl was hit by a piece of guitar and rushed to hospital in true 'Sally Simpson' style. Afterwards Townshend seemed more upset than the girl who felt 'quite honoured.' He gave her the guitar bits as a momento.
Despite playing live for the cameras, this is the one song which Townshend did not produce, and on which the Who did not play. Elton John's own band played on it and his record producer Gus Dudgeon produced it.
(Above left) John Entwistle 'guards' bass while (above right) Keith Moon slaughters drums and (left) Pete Townshend smashes guitar. Whilst waiting (far left) Townshend takes a small 'tipple' and surveys the audience.

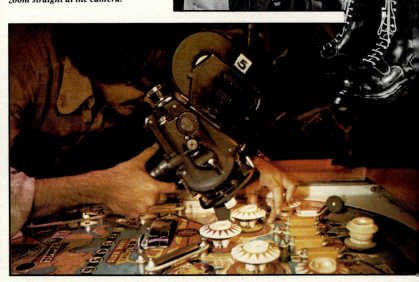

After three days hot, hectic and repetitive filming for 'Pinball Wizard', the 1,500 extras gave an emotional standing ovation to Ken Russell and crew.
(Left & Above) Elton gratefully stands on a box whenever his boots are not in camera. This scene with the crowd behind him is shown in film clip top right. Clapping, cheering and 'atmosphere' were recorded and mixed with Elton's studio tape giving it a 'live' feeling.
(Right) Elton tries out his huge new 'bovver-boots' for the first time.
(Below) Close-up shooting of pintable using a special prism lens which films at a 45° angle. The pinballs appear to zoom straight at the camera.

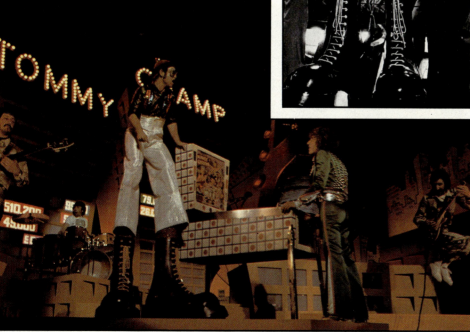

had to climb a step-ladder to put his boots on, or rather to be put ... s boots. But once strapped in (right) he could walk about with them. ...w) Tommy, the Pinball Wizard, battles with the Pinball Champ. The ... provide the musical backing. Originally the Who were going to appear ...s of scenes. Early on in the filming however, Roger doubted this ...m, and they all agreed. Roger and Pete, who wasn't overstruck with ...g anyway, persuaded Ken Russell to drop the idea. Apart from this ... with Elton John, the Who as a group make only two other appearances. ...e) The set was reassembled weeks later at Shepperton Studios to ...xtra close-ups. Director and star look tired and bored.

get it ready in time each day, especially as inevitably there had to be re-painting where sections had got knocked about in the move.

The scene required some 1,500 extras to pack the theatre in rival groups, one lot cheering Tommy and one lot the champ. Most of these came from the local technical college, and part of the deal was that their Student's Union would be allowed to film the making of the film. Robert Stigwood gave them some money for equipment. Also in payment to the extras and at their suggestion the Who gave a free concert for them when filming was finished—a concert Townshend considers one of the band's recent best.

With a mass of film equipment and crew and 1,500 extras packing a small provincial theatre, you have to take precautions against accident. The fire brigade and the St. John's ambulance people were constantly in attendance during filming, and although there were several people fainting and a few getting a bit crushed, there was only one real injury: it was when the Who are playing and the crowd had to storm the stage. The signal for this was Townshend smashing his guitar and throwing the neck up in the air, but one take he threw it a bit high, and it came down on a girl's head. "There was blood everywhere", remembers Townshend", and she was carried off to hospital. But she came back a few hours later and told us she was 'very honoured' to have been smashed over the head by Pete Townshend's guitar. I gave her the guitar". Shades of Sally Simpson.

Elton John's giant pinball machine came in for one of Ken Russell's sudden flashes of inspiration during filming. He wondered whether they could fit it with something that looked like a keyboard so Elton could play as he sang as he played pinball. They tried chrome studs at first, but it didn't look right, and then John Clark nipped down to Woolworths and bought a toy organ keyboard which they grafted on to the machine and pasted with glitter. Mr. Russell was pleased.

Filming the scene, they went through the song in short sections, over and over again, but when they'd finished the extras demanded they play the whole thing through. You'd think they'd have been sick to death with the thing, but they stomped and cheered at the end, and gave the director a standing ovation. Mr. Russell was moved.

For the Preacher's 'Eyesight To The Blind' section, Russell had the idea of staging it in a shrine dedicated to St. Marilyn, where the crippled and the blind come to worship images of Marilyn Monroe with the faith that they will be cured. "I used the Monroe images in that particular sequence to show how pop heroes can become defiled. It's something I'm particularly conscious of since the film I shot at Lourdes (one of his first, amateur, films) where people put a blind faith in graven images like the Bernadette statuette. It doesn't really matter to me if people get comfort from these kind of things —if their faith is strong enough, it may in fact cure. But it is difficult to distinguish between the divine and the commercial— who is to say whether Marilyn Monroe was less divine than Bernadette"? The scene involves a vast church hung with Marilyn portraits, a 10-foot statue of Marilyn on a rostrum towed by 10 girls in Marilyn masks, blond wigs, and costumes made from Marilyn photos and press clippings, with Eric Clapton strolling down the aisle doing 'Eyesight To The Blind' flanked by a slightly uncomfortable looking Pete Townshend and John Entwistle. "I've piddled about with acting, but I don't feel comfortable doing it", says Townshend. "I do most of my acting on the typewriter". If Clapton looks slightly bemused on the screen, it could be because he was, and it could also be that the brandy was flowing like canteen tea. Or as Townshend put it: "Everyone was pissed out of their brains that day. It was great to have Eric in the film and get him down there—it was all part of his coming out therapy".

For the extras playing the blind and crippled seekers after healing, they brought in genuinely blind and handicapped people—which inevitably will cause some controversy. Legend had it that the people hiring them assumed—this being a Ken Russell film—that they'd have to get authentic extras, but that Russell was mildly surprised when they all turned up. But then legend has a lot of things.

Pete Townshend again: "Obviously I didn't speak to them all but those I did speak to seemed happy to be in the film. Some said they identified with Tommy, feeling normal inside yet crippled outside. It was pretty gruelling for them, pretty hard work, but they could have quit any time they wanted to. A lot of them had listened to 'Tommy' and had much better credentials for getting a lift out of it than you or I".

The filming was done in a de-consecrated church in Portsmouth, but even so it caused problems—both within the unit and without. A local vicar got hot and bothered about it, and one of the Sunday papers ran one of those "Bearded Film Director Stages Hippie Pop Orgy In Church" stories: all it needed was senior citizen and a dog. In the sequence, when Tommy reaches the Marilyn statue to touch it, the graven image topples over and smashes into a thousand pieces. This meant they had to provide one robust Marilyn for the main shooting, which they made from fibreglass, and two plaster ones for smashing. The figure was too big to get through the door of the church, so the fibreglass one had to be made in sections and assembled inside. But the plaster ones had to be made on the spot—and then hidden from view while the rest of the filming was going on. And they were so fragile they couldn't be moved around a lot. They'd calculated that the statues would break at the knees, so Russell lined up the shot on that premise: they had two chances. Take one, the statue cracked . . . at the ankles. They missed the shot. Take two, they got it.

IN CASE you're getting the impression that 22 weeks in the life of the 'Tommy' movie was all problems and grumbling and narrowly-averted disaster, remember the exploits of Mr. Moon and Mr. Reed, which have already established themselves in the mythology of both rock and film business. Remember also the night Eric Clapton spent hammering on Ann-Margret's hotel-room door yelling "Ann-Margret I love you, I'm yours Ann-Margret". And remember the time some of the production's most valuable livewires decided to tease Harry Benn into wetting himself and reaching for the tranquilisers.

It was while the unit was based at Hayling Island on the South coast, and Pete Townshend had just bought a Grand Banks boat, which had been delivered and moored down there: To celebrate, Townshend took Moon, Ollie Reed and a few friends out to the boat for a bit of a party. They drove round the island for ages in Pete's Mercedes and Moony's Rolls, trying to remember where the boat had been moored, eventually found

(Left top) Clapton joking with photographers.
(Left middle) Arthur Brown gives 'communion'.
(Left bottom) Russell talks to some of the blind.
(Above left) Apprehensive Pete Townshend, John Entwistle and congregation follow 'preacher' Eric.
(Above right) The painter gives a final 'touch-up.'
(Below left) Blind follower kissing the statue.
(Below centre) The lighting cameraman; Dick Bush.
(Below right) A gaggle of Marylin Monroes rest.

The billowing clouds of incense, the swaying disciples in Marylin Monroe face masks, the repetition of John Entwistle's eerie bass-line and the atmospheric lighting of Dick Bush, all combined made filming 'Eyesight to the blind' a moody and weird occasion. In fact a sunday newspaper ran a 'Bearded Hippie Film Director Pop Orgy Sensation In Local Church Horror Drama' type of feature about it a few days later. The real stars of the filming were the disabled and blind extras. Their cheerfulness and stamina introduced both freshness and reality. Clapton had to wait ten hours before acting, but if he was a bit 'laid back' as the preacher, his guitar playing was most outstanding. "It was all part of his coming out" said Townshend Arthur Brown was later brought in successfully to pep up the proceedings but his singing wasn't included on the 'Tommy sound-track' record album.

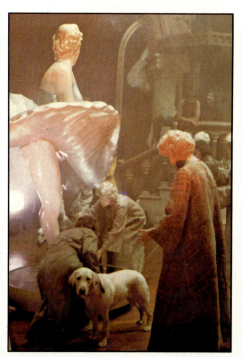  

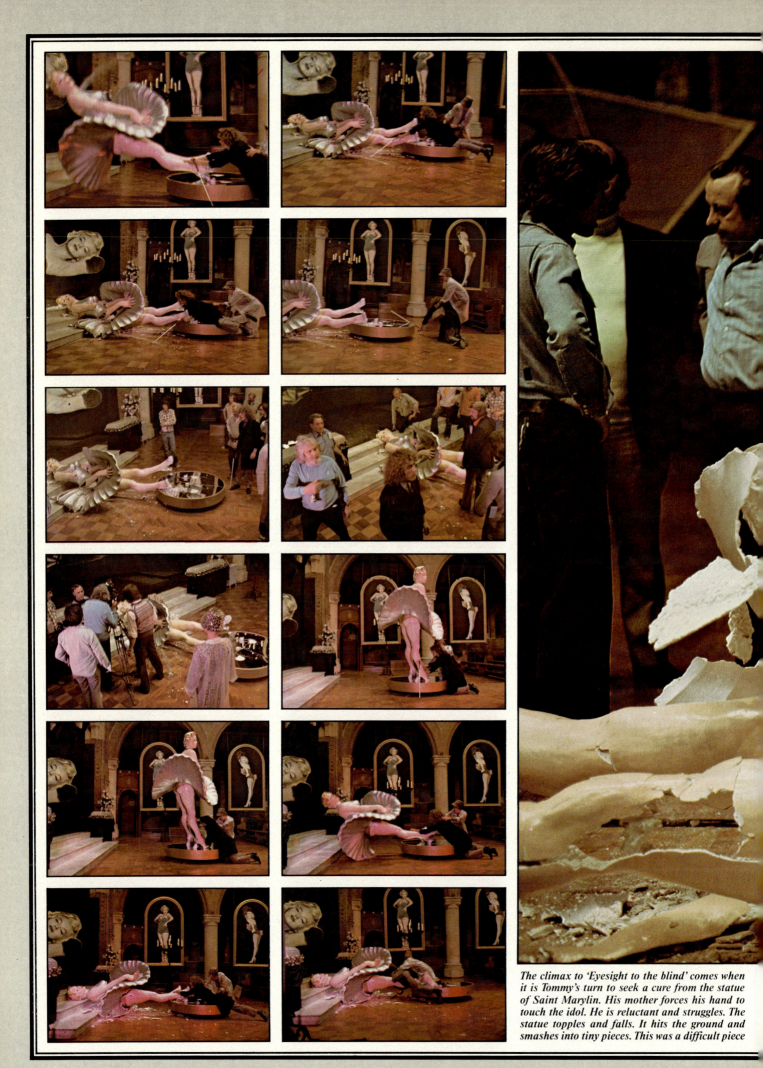

The climax to 'Eyesight to the blind' comes when it is Tommy's turn to seek a cure from the statue of Saint Marylin. His mother forces his hand to touch the idol. He is reluctant and struggles. The statue topples and falls. It hits the ground and smashes into tiny pieces. This was a difficult piece

of action to film and proved troublesome. As well as the main fibre-glass statue two others to be broken, were made in plaster. They calculated the statue would break at the knees, fall and land with it's head on the second step behind (see series of pictures). The first statue however broke at the ankles and landed in the wrong place. This meant that the high speed camera filming it in slow motion, missed the shot. After a discussion they set up the second statue in a different position. It smashed beautifully and was captured by all three cameras. Two statues are not enough for Russell who likes to have as many different 'takes' as he can get. (Above) Sitting and brooding deep in thought, he surveys the wreckage of the second statue – 'There's no more to play with today.' Not to worry, the footage he had, made a very dramatic ending to a scene that was rich in Russell symbolism.

it, borrowed a tender and rowed out clutching bottles of brandy and rum. Then the fun started—Moon set the tender adrift so they were marooned aboard, which was fine except he'd left a bottle of brandy in it. Then Moon decided he'd had enough and went up on deck: the others heard a splash and went up to find a little pile of clothes and no Moon.

They were desperately peering out across the water, Townshend getting more and more worried, when they heard a giggle, and found Moon shivering behind a mast. Later on, Ollie actually did jump in, but he got back aboard safely. Harry Benn, the associate producer, would have been a worried man if he thought his expensive stars were marooned in the middle of the Channel somewhere, so they decided to let him know—they sent out distress calls over the radio for an hour and a half . . . and no one heard or answered. The jokers really were marooned.

When morning came, Ollie and Moon swam back—going from buoy to buoy until they got ashore and were able to borrow another tender. Harry didn't need his tranquilisers.

HOWEVER MUCH can be laid at the director's door when things go over schedule or budget—and there is a strong argument that the original estimates were decidely unrealistic—it has to be remembered that especially on location the whole operation is largely dependent on luck. Perhaps that's why so many film people tend to be superstitious. The weather can prohibit filming for days at a time and accidents and Circumstances Beyond Our Control can cause frustrating delays and accountant's heart failure.

'Tommy' had its share of rough luck—not least some bouts of unfriendly weather. But there were two fairly spectacular incidents. You will recall that Ann-Margret has earned the nickname 'Slugger' for being accident prone, and that while she was making 'Tommy' she received damages of £620,000 for a serious fall she had at a Las Vegas nightclub: she had to have extensive plastic surgery, and she woke in hospital in a cast, with her jaw wired up, and covered in bandages. The same day that news of her award was announced, she was doing the 'Today It Rained Champagne' scene, in which she gets steadily drunker and drunker on champagne in a vast, white room as she watches her son on TV. It is Tommy's hour of triumph, he's become the pinball champion of the world and he is lionised by his followers, but his mother gets more and more depressed and maudlin thinking that all this means nothing to Tommy, the deaf, dumb and blind kid. The set is fantastic—all white drapes lit from the outside, and she feverishly switches channels on TV between the news and adverts for Rex Beans, Black Beauty chocolates, and soap powder. Finally she heaves a bottle through the television screen, and out floods first soap suds, then beans, then chocolate. It fills the room, and Ann-Margret wallows about in it.

On the set they'd got to the bit where soap suds are foaming out of the TV and filling the room. But then she starts to look a bit weird, and the foam around her starts

(Left) Ann-Margret runs riot in baked beans and almost turns 'Tommy' into a dirty film.
(Above) Foam filled the room and she was soon quite literally up to her neck in it. Unfortunately as she was dancing around she cut her hand on the jagged glass of the TV screen. The crew didn't realize until the foam turned pink and she turned white. She was hurriedly carried out (below) to a studio car which rushed her to the nearest hospital.
(Below right) Three hours and 24 stitches later she arrives back on set, her arm heavily bandaged.
(Right) The huge apparatus that causes all the mess is being tested. Tanks full of beans and chocolate empty down a chute to the TV set. Then they are forced out under pressure. 200 gallons of beans or chocolate pour from the TV screen with each tip.

going a bit pink. She'd cut her hand and arm on the jagged edge of the TV screen, was rushed to hospital, and had to have 24 stitches. The accident was carefully kept out of the Press at the time.

Apart from the anguish that caused the producers, it meant that one of the leading actors, who appears right through the film, was out of action while the wound healed. The unit had had great difficulty booking hotels in the lake district in peak holiday season, and now filming there had to be put back two weeks and all the bookings changed. Somehow they managed it—but it wasn't one of Fate's kindlier acts.

Then of course there was Southsea Pier—which burned out during filming in a blaze of painted woodwork and publicity. It was a beautiful old wooden building, still in use as a theatre at the resort, which they'd chosen as the location for the ballroom at Bernie's Holiday Camp, where Nora begins to melt into Frank's arms. Somehow, a small fire started while they were there, and the fire brigade were called, but as the building was entirely made of wood the fire spread before it could be brought under control and the theatre was completely gutted. They kept the cameras running through the whole thing, and Russell even used some of the footage in 'Tommy' during the final scenes where Tommy runs through the burning pintables and on to the beach

It was an expensive accident—both in goodwill (the unit wasn't vastly popular in Southsea after that, and they still had several scenes to shoot there) and in compensation for the extras. The wardrobe van had been caught by the blaze, and many of the extras lost their belongings. The claims they put in shed a strange light on the sort of things film extras carry around with them. They ranged from meticulous people who'd claim for a pair of plimsolls worth 95p and a jacket worth £2 with half a packet of wine gums in the pocket, to the other extreme. The film company suddenly realised that some of their extras were among the best dressed in the country—owners of Astrakan coats with bulging wallets and expensive sunglasses in the pockets.

The accountants had to smile as they signed the compensation cheques.

IN NUTSHELL form, Ken Russell's object for film-making is: "To entertain first, and the preaching comes secondary. Most of my films are based on that premise". It seems simple enough, but the concept of the film director as entertainer conceals a seething mass of details which would be enough to daunt the most ardent of people. The skeletal outline is clear enough: having assembled your crew, worked out your schedule, got your cast, found your locations and made sure you have people around you to look after forseeable problems, you point the camera and make the film. Nothing is ever as simple as that, but as the man at the head of this vast army the director-as-general has a responsibility to ensure the headaches are as mild as possible. Apart from laying in sacks of aspirin, how does he do it?

It's a wonder there aren't more directors with acute schizophrenia: people talk wryly about the difference between Russell wearing

Ann-Margret hasn't eaten beans since the time she had to roll around 6" deep in them (above).
(Above right) Ken Russell covers her with yet another bucketful, and many more follow (right). This fantasy sequence had gallons of soap suds, baked beans and liquid chocolate pour out of a TV set. At first masses of the stuff was made up by colouring soya beans and cornflour. It all went bad when filming was postponed because of Ann-Margret's accident (page 59). Real beans and chocolate were eventually used. During filming two valuable rings, lost by Ann-Margret, were recovered when over 4,000 lbs of beans from the studio floor were carefully sieved by hand.

his producer's hat and Russell the extravagant, creative film maker. It's hardly surprising he explodes under the pressure.

He has a basic method in that he keeps his main crew as much a family affair as possible: wherever he can he'll use people with whom he's worked before—from the actors to the continuity assistant. People suggest that he likes to get the measure of people, and often hires them because they're not likely to outshine him, or people he knows he can shout at with impunity. That charge may be unfair, though there may be an element of that in his reasoning: what is probably more important is the 'devil you know' idea. He's not a man to hire incompetents, even if they are submissive, but there could hardly be anything worse than finding out after a couple of days shooting that you've got a 'difficult' actor who'll put your schedule late with every tantrum, or a key member of your technical team who'll spend more time arguing than getting the job done. He's quite careful about picking new people, as John Clark's account of how he came to be the Art Director on 'Tommy' shows.

Clark was working with the Associate Producer, Harry Benn (a long-standing Russell clan member) on another film while they were setting up the 'Tommy' deal, and at that time Russell wasn't sure that he needed an art director to interpret his ideas. One interesting thing about Russell is that he can't draw—he can see everything in his head, but can't get it onto paper and he relys on his wife Shirley and a friend, Paul Dufficey, to translate for him. Harry Benn was pushing for Clark, but neither Russell nor Clark was sure: there were meetings, which as Clark describes them sound like fairly amicable fencing bouts, with each side retiring occasionally to think about the other. Eventually Russell asked him to join, and Clark agreed: "I said I would as long as it was clearly understood that I'm in charge of what I'm responsible for". He didn't want to risk being accused of falling down on the job when someone else had been meddling. Clark's no-nonsense attitude and Assistant Art Director Terry Snow's assertion that Russell likes to surround himself with talented people "on the way up", would appear to belie the charge that Russell prefers meek yes-men. Clark also said to him: "I hear you're not the kindest man on the floor"—another often-quoted thread of the Ken Russell legend. He is reputed to have a most ferocious temper on the set.

Pete Townshend: "As a man he's very warm and gentle with a large family he loves. But what happens is occasionally he lets go in the way I do sometimes on stage or when Moon and I go into one of our numbers in a hotel: his eyes start to roll and his head shakes and he goes out of control, and in many ways I think he enjoys it, it's a release for his frustration and suppressed energy". Townshend had but one nasty moment with the Russell temper: he was having a slight contretemps with the film sound people, which they were taking personally, when Russell intervened: "All I said very quietly was: 'Don't shout at me mate,' and he dropped his voice and it was over". Ollie

The luxurious and clean white room (top left) as Nora starts to have a nervous breakdown.
Determined not to be the only one covered in beans, Ann-Margret attacks Ken Russell. He retaliates and a light hearted bean-fight (top right and centre) breaks out between them on the set.
Camera and crew were protected from flying chocolate and beans by plastic sheeting (above left). The lens was fitted with a special 'window' which had to be wiped down after each take (left).
Robert Stigwood, Tommy's producer, makes one of his rare appearances on the set. (above).
The near-impossible task of cleaning up the set for filming to re-start with the room clean (right).

Reed tends to take him quietly aside. The moral seems to be that if you allow yourself to be trodden on, the director will tread. 'Tommy' saw two assistant directors come and go after Russell had bawled them out in front of a crowd, but with the third he met his match. Jonathon Benson had a calm, upper-crust BBC cool and he wouldn't let Russell's outbursts ruffle him. "Ken just wouldn't give him any nonsense", said one observer. "He was in a world of his own, did his job, and Russell just didn't get angry with him".

Russell's method as a director is full of contradictions. He's a film director who doesn't like to direct actors (another reason he likes people he knows and who know him) and prefers them to follow his basic idea more or less by intuition while he gets on with the more technical aspects: he likes to use the camera himself a lot. He's a man who encourages anyone from the leading actor to the clapper boy to come to him with ideas, yet he can be as dictatorial as the next man, going through take after take after take to get exactly the shot he wants. He hates the whole movie industry showbusiness charade, and much prefers to leave studios alone and shoot on location; yet he also has his Cecil B. De Mille streak of extravagance. He writes his own scripts and is as conscious as anyone of budgets and time, yet he constantly re-writes and changes as new ideas occur to him while he's shooting. Especially with a musical, this can wreak havoc with the schedules. Though the soundtrack had been completed in advance of shooting, Russell allowed his inspiration to take him far away from his original ideas in several sections.

It can happen by the merest chance: there's one whole sequence where, in the original script, people leave their office desks and factory benches, come out from behind bank counters, even walk off military parades as Tommy's message is piped through public address systems by Frank and Uncle Ernie—the basic idea being to show how the Tommy evangelism was getting out of control. Russell dropped the scenes but in the film Daltrey glides over various scenes and the people change, feel the power as he passes by. Hell's Angels stop fighting and dance, Teds in a cafe stop loafing round the gambling machines and dance, blind people line up outside a home and look up as he passes. The Hell's Angels got in there through Shirley Russell advertising for a leather coat for Cousin Kevin to wear during his tormentor sequence, and someone from a group called the Shagrats sent in a fantastic garment, completely covered in motor-cycle badges: it was too late for Cousin Kevin, but by way of the Shagrats, Shirley and Ken got to know a really tough bunch of Angels who impressed Russell so much that he wrote them into the film.

Improvising on the script like that not only put days, and eventually weeks, on the time the film takes to shoot, but involved Pete Townshend in an enormous amount of extra work, locked in the studio for twelve hours a day, seven days a week, changing and adapting the soundtrack to fit what Russell had actually filmed. This inspirational approach to filming has financiers

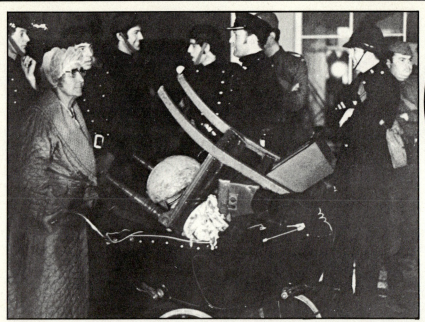
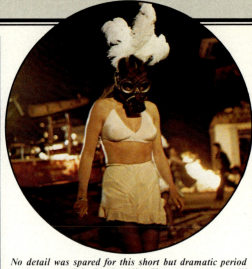

No detail was spared for this short but dramatic period setting scene of the London blitz. These sequences, up till "It's a boy" were originally going to be in black and white. (Left) Extras dressed as firemen, policemen and ARP wardens. (Above) Typically Russell: Satin, feathers and gas-masks. (Right) Captain Walker and Nora uncover a dead boy's body. (Below) Two cars and a whole street were set alight. The period fire engine, doing its second blitz, is still in use.

pulling their hair out and caused a certain amount of animosity amongst the crew, but is also part of the reason Russell makes great films rather than being merely a good man on the production line.

Set gossip also centered around his habit of doing a great many takes of each scene, and then—after taking something 13 or 14 times—often using the second or third one. There is obviously method in his eccentricity—first that he likes to provide himself with as much raw material as he can get by the time he comes to the editing stage, and secondly that he likes to be sure to get it right. This is his perfectionism. Perhaps the most extreme example was on part of the "I'm Free" section which involved Daltrey running through a field of bright yellow mustard flowers. Russell had Daltrey run through that mustard field 32 times before he was satisfied, and there's nothing much you can do wrong filming a man running across a field. That day his reputation as Ken "just one more last take" Russell was firmly entrenched. The advantages for him are obvious, but the disadvantages are that people get bored and tired and lose their enthusiasm for the scene if they have to go through it over and over and over again. In another shot, Daltrey had to run through a commando training course and get thrown in a judo fall by one of the soldiers: they did it again until eventually Daltrey made a mistake in the way he fell and was out cold for half an hour or so.

But Russell proved with the Acid Queen shots with Tina Turner, that he could get it together in just a few takes. Tina Turner simply had to leave the country after a couple of days because she had other committments, so Russell knew that if he wanted her in his film it had to be done fast: the crew hardly knew what had hit them as the scenes were shot and finished in swift succession in a couple or four takes.

Perfectionism isn't merely the director's prerogative, naturally. One of the most staggering things about a production on the scale of 'Tommy' is the amount of time, money and trouble that is spent setting up and filming scenes that will last a matter of seconds or minutes in the actual film. They'd spend a whole day filming in exactly the right location with hundreds of extras to get just a few shots for the ballroom section of Bernie's Holiday Camp, where Nora Walker is falling in love with Frank. It's just part of the section where she takes Tommy to the camp, meets Frank, dances with him, goes swimming, enters the Lovely Legs competition, wins, and goes home with Frank as Tommy's new Uncle—but every part has to be right. One of the opening shots in the film is where Nora and Captain Walker are running in their evening clothes through a blitzed street: setting up and filming that scene seems, to the outsider, to take an almost unbelievably disproportionate amount of trouble compared to the amount of time it is on the screen.

There was an area of Portsmouth that was being demolished and the local council were persuaded to leave a couple of streets to be blitzed by the film crew. In this context, set dressing takes on a whole new meaning: the art direction team got busy, knocking away bits of houses with the help of a man with a bulldozer and a ball and chain: Nobby Clarke started work with his gas jets and paraffin rags, preparing the fire effects, and the idea of real explosions was tried and rejected: the props department took immense care in getting period cars in the street ready to be overturned and set alight, placing the right kind of curtains, ornaments and furniture in the houses—and as every collector knows, Thirties and Forties stuff is fetching a fair price at the moment. They got a period fire engine, which is still in working order as a reserve for the Hampshire fire brigade, dressed the extras in ARP uniforms and clothes of the time, rehearsed little incidental pieces of action—like some people being rescued from a burning house—which probably wouldn't be noticed in the film because you're looking at Ann-Margret running through in a ball gown, organised emergency fire and ambulance services to be on standby in case of accidents, and dealt with the fears of nearby local residents. They were going to film through the night, and a local deputation came to point out that there were old people in the area who might be frightened by explosions.

Actually to film it, they had to use a battery of carbon lamps which introduce yet another complication into each take: the lamps burn rods of carbon, which frizzle as they give out a fierce, bright light. Before each take the chief electrician has to check with the man on each lamp that the rod is long enough to last, and if not they have to wait while he turns off the lamp, unscrews the rod, puts another one in . . . if they're all going out at different times, one detail like that can prove incredibly complicating.

Building Uncle Ernie's organ was another example of a great deal of trouble and expense for a very short time on celluloid. It is a fantastic creation—a huge organ-cum-cash register built on the chassis of a Mini Moke which Uncle Ernie plays at the entrance to Tommy's holiday camp. They tried all sorts of ways to do it, including mounting the construction on a milk float, but as it had to go uphill at a fair lick, they decided to use a petrol engine. It took weeks to build it, and in the end was something of a rush job because it was needed on the set, and instead of moulding it out of fibreglass it had to be done in plywood, which isn't as flexible as the designers would have liked. They had to hire a man from the maker to drive it, because none of the crew was prepared to squash in sideways and work the rather oddly-positioned controls. Squashed in beside the driver was another geezer who had to operate the cash-register mechanism. Originally, the machine was going to be featured quite heavily in the film but as the emphasis for devilry switched from Uncle Ernie to Frank, so did the opportunities for using the Organ. It was an expensive toy: four and a half thousand pounds for one scene. It is now resting in the props department at Pinewood.

One final Russell idosyncrasy: traditionally while shooting, the director looks at the previous day's rushes every morning, but although the rushes are always shown on a Russell film, neither the director nor the actors go to see them. Thus on 'Tommy' it was some time before he realised that several sequences had been shot out of focus because of a defective lens. They had to be shot again.

JUST AS work goes on before shooting starts, so it goes on when all that is finished. Each scene has to be edited into shape and to the correct length to fit the music, or the music has to be altered to fit the scene, the whole thing has to be strung together, the special effects have to be done, and the sound has to be dubbed.

Film Editor Stuart Baird used to work while the film was still being shot: he'd get

61

Do you think it's alright
To leave the boy with cousin Kevin?
Do you think it's alright?
There's something about him I don't really like
Do you think it's alright?
I think it's alright
I think it's alright

We're on our own cousin, all alone, cousin
Let's think of a game to play
Now the grown-ups have all gone away
You wont be much fun,
Being blind, deaf and dumb,
But I've no one to play with today
D'you know how to play hide and seek?
To find me it would take you a week,
But tied to that chair you wont go anywhere
There's a lot I can do to a freak

How would you feel if I turned on the bath
Ducked your head under and started to laugh
Maybe a cigarette burn on your arm
Would change your expression to one of alarm

I'm the school bully!
The classroom cheat
The nastiest playfriend,
You ever could meet
I'll put glass in your dinner
And spikes in your seat...

COUSIN KEVIN

I'm the school bully!
The classroom cheat,
The nastiest playfriend,
You ever could meet
I'll stick pins in your fingers
And tread on your feet

I'll drag you around by a lock of your hair
And give you a push at the top of the stairs
What would you do if I shut you outside
To stand in the rain and catch cold so you died?

We're on our own, cousin, all alone, cousin
We thought up some nice games to play
While the grown-ups had all gone away
You weren't too much fun,
'Cos you're blind, deaf and dumb
But I've no one to play with today

together the rushes and do a rough cut of the scene which he'd then show to Russell: on 'Tommy' Russell and Baird seemed generally to agree—there were no major alterations to Baird's initial ideas, which is another example of Russell liking his key people to contribute their own ideas to the project and of the sympathy between the director and his team. Like everyone else, Baird has his reservations about 'Tommy', but he is particularly pleased with his work on the Sally Simpson sequence, which is very sharp and makes its point well in quite a short time.

Dubbing the sound proved to be a rather complex procedure which eventually took four months or so. They had to do several different mixes—one for the quintaphonic system, one stereo, one mono, and one double-stereo which is mainly for cinemas in America which like to use stereo with an extra pair of speakers at the back. The mix in each case is different to suit the possibilities of each system, and the technique of mixing music to go with the images on the screen in any case is different from mixing for records. Pete Townshend became quite closely involved with the process, and early on learnt the differences between record and cinema: the film sound people also say that they learnt a lot from working with 'Tommy'. To mix for the quintaphonic system, they had to bring in three mixing decks and have one in the dead centre of the dubbing theatre—sometimes there were more than 50 music tracks to be assembled.

It was an extremely long and hard process, which involved them working long hours—even late on Christmas Eve. As it happened, they were working on the Christmas sequence that night, and things started to get a little crazy: Townshend and the technicians were slaving away while Russell went out for a break, and he came back to find they'd decorated the dubbing theatre with paper chains, and were sitting there in rabbit masks. They all turned to look at him—he took one glance and went home.

"IT'S OBVIOUSLY difficult for me to be objective", says Pete Townshend, "But I remember getting a chill up my spine after seeing rushes of the 'Acid Queen' sequence. Tina Turner is so right for the role (remember his original idea was to have Tiny Tim?) and she brings to the part that aggressive feminine thing that chills you in the same way that parts of 'The Exorcist' chill. It was the only sequence that the censors were particularly worried about—they seemed to think it was pure horror, although apart from the snakes in the skeleton there is nothing very nasty visually. It's really Tina's portrayal that's so terrifying—her face".

The Acid Queen is a sinister mix of Soho sleaze, drug mythology and urban voodoo: Tommy is taken to her in the desperate (and vain) hope that she can cure him. She doesn't, but she leaves her mark.

The Acid Queen is Tina Turner: it is also a complicated mass of tubes, syringes, lights, mirrors and fibreglass that cost a lot both in heartache and money. It was Shirley Russell's idea: it came to her in a restaurant one day, and she made a rough sketch of it there, and then a full colour design, which she passed to John Clark who made the working drawings and got the thing made. The idea was to have some kind of sinister machine—all lights and mirrors—with syringes pointing through to the inside. Tina Turner does her dance, is dressed in a cloak and has a helmet put on her head: the helmet is the head of the Acid Queen (or the Iron

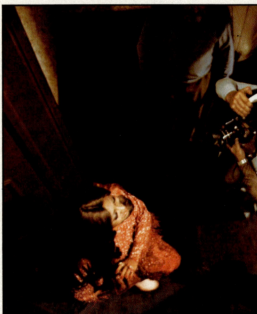
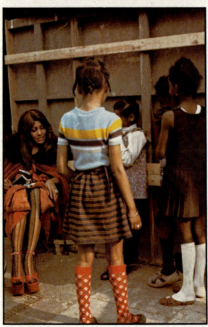

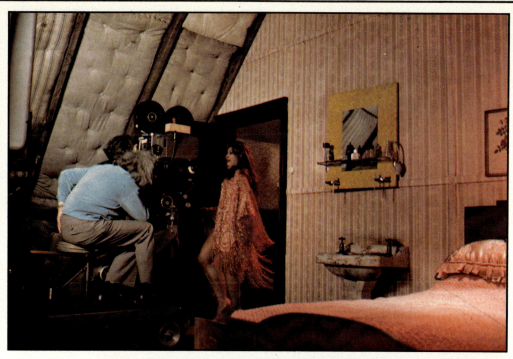

Choosing Tina Turner for the part of the 'Acid Queen' was a piece of 'mastercasting' by Robert Stigwood: Her face expresses just the right combination of lust and menace. Her fast sinuous dancing brings out all the power, excitement and horror of the song. She had to keep to a tight schedule, so flew into England one day, recorded her song at the Who's Ramport studio the next, filmed for four more, then left for a U.S. concert. Russell therefore had no time to get over-involved or bogged down. The scene was one of the fastest filmed, and one of the best. (Top and left) Nifty hand-held camerawork was needed as the 'Acid Queen' danced and glided in and out of Tommy's nightmare. (Far left) Attended by handmaidens in her attic hovel. Filming in the small, crowded mattress-lined room was hot and unbearable. (Below left) Shy and awestruck little girls talk to Tina Turner during a coffee-break. Just as Russell was satisfied with a 'take' outside the sleazy strip club (below), it was noticed that a dog had been sitting in view. Both dog and Russell seem bewildered. (Right) The sinister beauty of the 'Acid Queen.'

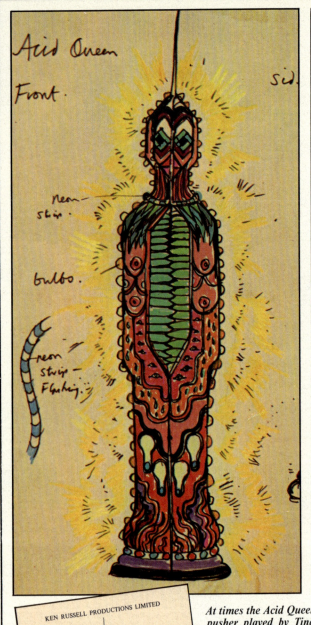

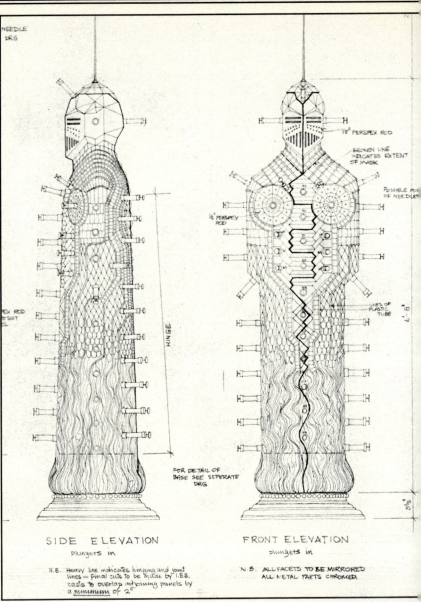

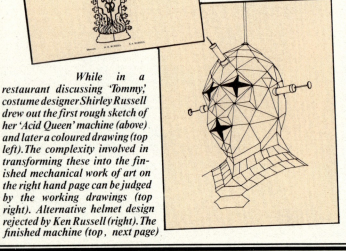

At times the Acid Queen was no lady: The dancing hooker/pusher played by Tina Turner changed from woman to machine. The machine was designed so that when someone was placed inside they were injected with a coloured drug through its 68 syringes. Tommy was its victim and we catch glimpses of his different painful and pleasurable hallucinations, as the machine opens and closes during his 'trip'. The 'Iron Maiden' as the machine was called, was the invention of costume designer Shirley Russell (Ken's missus). It was the film's most spectacular 'prop' and proved to be the most troublesome to construct. Unfortunately its real beauty is not apparent on the screen and it looks, at times, more like a flimsy scale-model, instead of an 8 ft. mirrored monster costing over £10,000. The fibre-glass body, supported by a steel frame, is covered with chrome and mirror. It could spin, light up and fill and empty the syringes, all by remote control. Roger Daltrey wanted to buy it when shooting was completed. (Right) Working on the Iron Maiden. (Far right) Ken Russell considers a worm's eye view. A copy of the machine without working parts was made in the U.S. for publicity and promotion purposes

While in a restaurant discussing 'Tommy,' costume designer Shirley Russell drew out the first rough sketch of her 'Acid Queen' machine (above) and later a coloured drawing (top left). The complexity involved in transforming these into the finished mechanical work of art on the right hand page can be judged by the working drawings (top right). Alternative helmet design rejected by Ken Russell (right). The finished machine (top, next page)

66

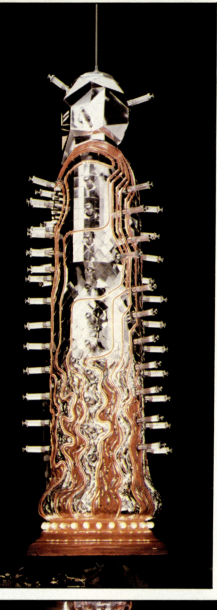
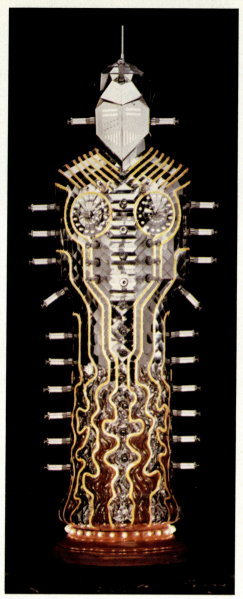
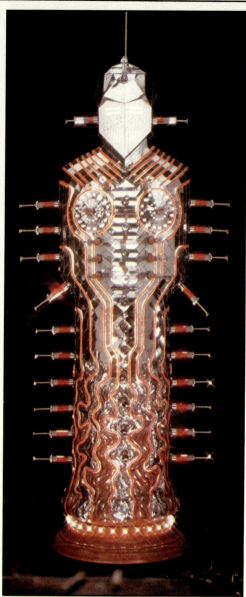

Maiden as it became known on the set) and she metamorphoses into the machine. Tommy gets inside the machine and the needles inject him with thousands of shots of a well-known hallucinogen. As he goes through his acid experience, the front of the machine opens to show him in various fantasies—as Jesus covered with poppies, as a skeleton with snakes crawling over and through him, dressed in a loincloth, in the guise of his father...

There were other ideas: he was to be covered in butterflies, but that didn't work out: and in ants. Originally, the snakes were to be crawling all over Daltrey, but one of the handlers got bitten early on, and they decided not to risk it and used the skeleton instead. Then when they counted the snakes afterwards they found they were one short, but the handlers were confident it would die in the cold of the night. Days later they found it, curled up in an inaccessible corner of the machine, still alive—Daltrey had been in and out of the machine several times while it was still there. Ken Russell, incidentally, is terrified of snakes and spent the whole time up a step ladder, brandishing a stout stick and with his trousers tucked into his socks.

Designing and making the Acid Queen was a major headache for Art Director John Clark: it had to stand up to some pretty heavy treatment—spinning round and round on a Rolls Royce turntable while filled with coloured liquids, the front having to open and close continually, having to withstand the heat of lights both outside and inside. Originally the plan was to shoot it in three days, after which it could fall apart if it wished, but shooting dragged on over several weeks in the event, so the machine was subjected to much rougher tests than had been anticipated. Originally it was to be faced with coloured plastic, but then that was changed to mirrors which put extra strain on the fibreglass superstructure—and the superstructure turned out not to be strong enough anyway.

Clark admits that was partly his fault: he was trying to supervise the construction of the thing while he was in Portsmouth, and at that distance he wasn't able to check that his specification of at least 3/16ths of an inch had been observed. When he got back he found that it was much thinner. The machine was an adventurous experiment, and has produced a remarkable film effect—but it wasn't without a welter of teething problems and exasperation. Russell would get madder and madder as the fibreglass would shift position and the front wouldn't open and close properly, and Clark and his team would be dashing around trying to sort it out.

But as he says, John Clark had an unanswerable comeback: "But Ken", he'd reason. "I've never made an Acid Queen before. Have you"?

Do you think it's alright
To leave the boy with Uncle Ernie?
Do you think it's alright?
He's had a few too many tonight
Do you think it's alright?
I think it's alright
Yes, I think it's alright

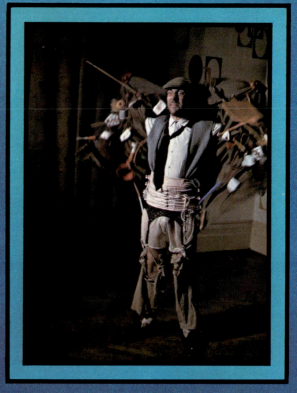

I'm your wicked Uncle Ernie
I'm glad you won't see or hear me
As I fiddle about
Fiddle about
Fiddle about…
Your mother left me here to mind you,
And I'm doing exactly what I bleedin' well want to
Fiddling about
Fiddling about
Fiddle about

fiddle about

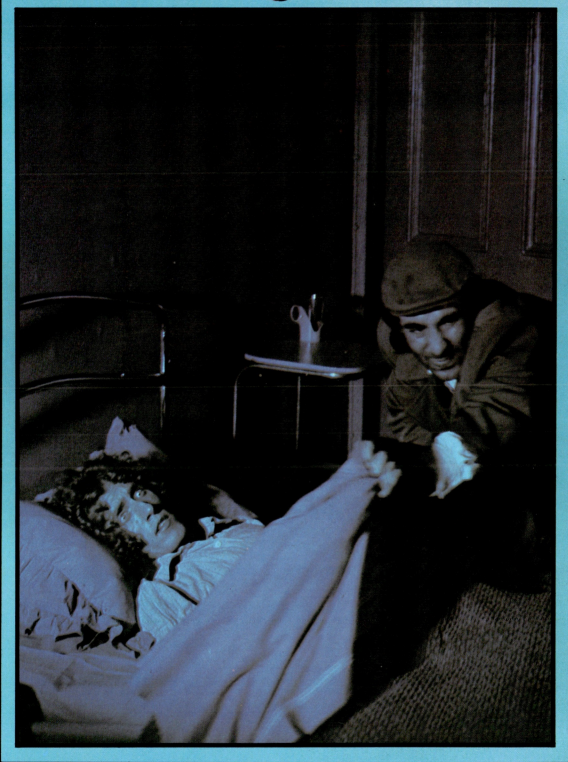

Down with your bedclothes
Up with your nightshirt!
Fiddle about
Fiddle about
Fiddle about!
You won't shout as I fiddle about
Fiddle about
Fiddle about
Fiddle about
Aaaaaaaaaaah!

The day after the blaze, the local paper, THE NEWS had coloured pictures of the burning pier on its front page (above). It carried a special 'Disaster-Supplement' (right). (Top left) Filming inside the beautiful ornate ballroom. (Top right) Oliver Reed and dancers spot the smoke. (Top) A picture-postcard of the pier before the fire destroyed it.

A tragic and di trous fire broke o the ballroom Southsea pier du the filming of Tom Oliver Reed and Margret were dan for a part of "Bernie's Ho Camp" song. Sudd smoke was seen con from a curtain and of the ceiling ca alight. The ballroom evacuated and the crew tackled the fla The fire brigade ar but failed to contain fire and it spread ove wooden building. column of smoke cou seen for miles. Huna more firemen arrived a lifeboat and air rescue helicopter stood Although there were serious casualities, fire wearing oxygen-brea equipment had to re two others who were tra when part of the roof lapsed in flames. The crew had a lot of their eq ment and costumes destre many extras had their clo ruined. Ken Russell filme whole thing and a glimpse is included in the film. mayor of Portsmouth sa was "...a calamity – We have a landmark which was o the finest pier buildings or south coast. (Top right) T collapses and a holidaym moves deckchair to quieter

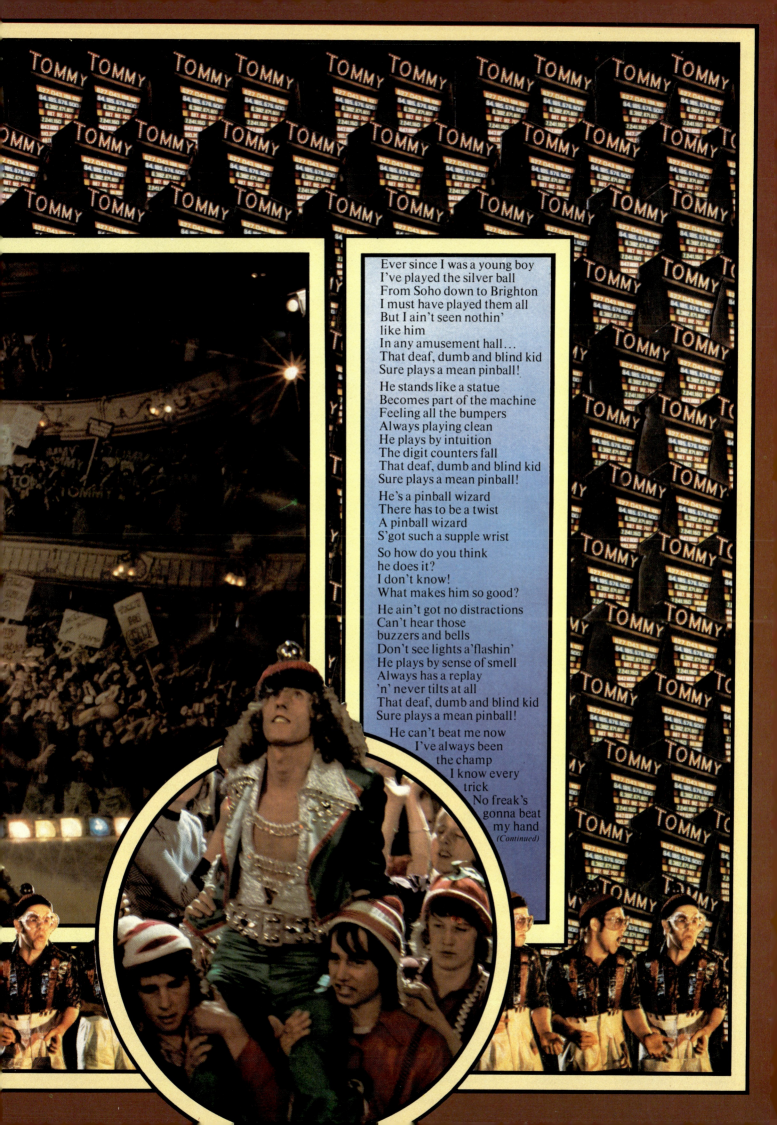

Ever since I was a young boy
I've played the silver ball
From Soho down to Brighton
I must have played them all
But I ain't seen nothin'
like him
In any amusement hall…
That deaf, dumb and blind kid
Sure plays a mean pinball!

He stands like a statue
Becomes part of the machine
Feeling all the bumpers
Always playing clean
He plays by intuition
The digit counters fall
That deaf, dumb and blind kid
Sure plays a mean pinball!

He's a pinball wizard
There has to be a twist
A pinball wizard
S'got such a supple wrist

So how do you think
he does it?
I don't know!
What makes him so good?

He ain't got no distractions
Can't hear those
buzzers and bells
Don't see lights a'flashin'
He plays by sense of smell
Always has a replay
'n' never tilts at all
That deaf, dumb and blind kid
Sure plays a mean pinball!

He can't beat me now
I've always been
the champ
I know every
trick
No freak's
gonna beat
my hand
(Continued)

Even on my usual table
He can beat my best
His disciples lead him in
And he just does the rest
He's got crazy flipper fingers
Never seen him fall
That deaf, dumb and blind kid
Sure plays a mean pinball!

He's a pinball wizard
There has to be a twist
A pinball wizard
S'got such a suppple wrist
Ooooooooooooooaaaaaah!

He's a pinball wizard
He's scored a trillion more
A pinball wizard
The World's new pinball Lord
He's scoring more…
He's scoring more!

I thought I was
The Bally table king
But I just handed
My pinball crown to him
To him. To him

Champagne

Today it rained champagne
A son was born again
A genius unchained
A life of wealth and fame,
wealth and fame

Champagne flowing down just like rain,
Caviar breakfasts every day
Merchant bankers and yachts at Cannes
Servants and cars and private sand

See me, feel me, touch me, heal me
See me, feel me, touch me, heal me,
heal me

They flock in thousands strong
We'll just play along
A million in reserve
For our love a just deserve, just deserve
Francs and dollars and peacock's wings
Sequinned gowns and birds that sing
Private planes
And fishing lakes
Bigger crowds and
bigger, bigger
takes

But what's it
all worth, what's it all worth
When my son is blind
He can't hear the music
Nor enjoy what I'm buying
His life is worthless
Affecting mine
I'd pay any price
To drive his plight from my mind

See me, feel me, Touch me, heal me
See me, feel me, Touch me, heal me

Roger Daltrey wasn't really thrown through plate-glass, it was 'all done by mirrors' – two mirrors in fact – and some clever editing. He was thrown at mirror no. 1 by Ann-Margret (above). Then the camera was stopped and mirror no. 2 (the broken one) set up. Daltrey resumed his position and the camera restarted. Bits of plastic were dropped behind the mirror to resemble flying glass. He jumped backwards through the mirror onto a mattress (left and below). When the two shots were joined, it looked as if he had been thrown straight through the first mirror. A brief cut away to Ann-Margret's horrified face hid the join, so although the actual moment of impact appears to be seen, it is not, it is only heard.

For the 'I'm Free' sequence Russell used a special-effect known as 'travelling matte.' Roger was filmed, against a blue-lit screen, running on a motorised endless belt (top). From the resulting film (left circle) two black & white copies were made using special film which is sensitive only to blue light. On one, is a black silhouette of Roger's running figure on clear film (centre circle). This is placed in contact with footage of the chosen background and the two are printed together. As each frame is copied the black silhouette of Roger prevents that portion from being exposed. This gives the 'prepared background' with a shape of clear unexposed film cut out of each frame which exactly corresponds to Roger's silhouette. The other black and white print (far circle) is used in the same way to mask out the blue from the original film, giving a copy of Roger running against a white background. When this is finally combined along with the 'prepared background' we get the desired effect of Roger apparently running as part of the background scene (right). It's a complicated effect. The results aren't always perfect as a look at some early shots used for pages 94 & 95 will show.

Some effects meant Roger had to quite literally 'put his back into it.' Tommy falls through space and into water after crashing through the mirror. To film this, Daltrey had to drop 20 ft. from a diving board (above) and land on his back with his arms outstretched. Pieces of plastic representing bits of shattered mirror were thrown in the air to float down with him. (Below) The wardrobe master taped a thick towel to Daltrey's back to cushion the impact when he landed, but as there were over twenty attempts to get this shot perfect, his back still got fairly bruised. A tricky technical problem is overcome when assistant director Johnathon Benson reads the light-meter, tied to the end of a pole, held out by lighting cameraman Ronnie Taylor.

Rare pictures of Roger Daltrey drowning (above and right). After falling through the mirror into water, Tommy is seen in slow-motion underwater. This, another tricky shot, was filmed with the camera behind the observation window of a swimming pool. In order to sink lower and rise slower, Roger Daltrey emptied his lungs of air before jumping in. On this occasion he swallowed a lot of water and was struggling to get out. The cameras were still running until it occurred to everyone that he was in trouble. Three people jumped in and pulled him out. In Hollywood days, an incident like this would have been exploited for publicity, but the many 'mishaps' that occurred while filming 'Tommy' were deliberately kept out of the press for fear of 'over-exposure'.

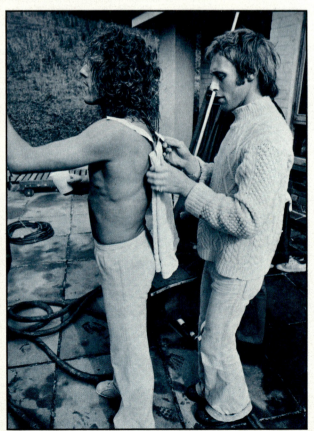

Ken Russell's final scene has its climax when Tommy climbs a mountain to sing, "Listening to you" and to raise his arms "... as if to embrace the life-giving sun." To give the impression of sunlight streaming through his hair, Roger Daltrey had to stand with his face inches away from a powerful lamp (right). Towels were again used to protect him, this time to stop his face and chest getting burned by the lamp (left). Careful positioning (left) meant that he obscured the lamp from the camera (above). The filmed scene (below) had a huge orange sun added later as a studio effect, the same one that opened the movie, bringing it round full circle.

With Oliver Reed and Keith Moon together on location there were m[any] moments of lunacy. It was probably no accident that their hotel was 15 m[iles] away from unit HQ. With all the stars, 'Who' people, and film technic[ians] coming and going they held an almost-continuous party. Russell was [so] vexed that Ollie Reed had eaten all the cockles from their favourite sea-s[ide] pub. Apparently Ollie walked straight from the pub into the sea, disappea[red] and then returned, soaking wet and placed a handful of cockles on the [bar] saying, "There you are, Jesus" (his favourite name for Russell). Mooney was his usual lovable outrageous self. Together they created a new 'low[est]' entertainment (below) when they did an impromtu concert in the studio [.] (Top row left) Sally Simpson alias Victoria Russell (Ken's daughter) frighte[ned] other diners with her scar, while Keith Moon (2nd pic top row) just frighte[ned] other diners. (Pics 3, 4 & 5) Russell didn't know that they had switched on [the] camera as he rehearsed a sailors hornpipe. Ollie Reed (Top row pics 6, [7, 8]) was voted 'Britain's sexiest actor' by readers of a magazine while ma[king] Tommy. (Pic 9) At last, photographic evidence that Townshend is 'up the p[ole]'. Unit photographer Graham Attwood couldn't resist taking this pictur[e of] Britain's sexiest drummer; Keith Moon. (Right) After some hectic lun[ch] P. C. Townshend sleeps it off on the floor. (Below right) Uncle Ernie disp[lays] his huge organ. This fabulous organ-cum-cash register could drive abou[t at] 25 mph. Moon wanted to buy it and turn it into a mobile drinks cab[inet]

Daltrey leaps spectacularly from the stage during the filming of 'Sally Simpson' (above). The pile of mattresses (right) made this a fairly safe and uneventful stunt. But others made up for it. For Daltrey the film often seemed like a 6 month obstacle course: Not only was he burned (p.46) and nearly drowned (p.78) he was once knocked unconscious for half an hour when he landed wrongly after a judo throw. Russell insisted on over 30 takes of a scene for 'I'm Free' where Tommy ran across a mustard field. His feet were so blistered afterwards that he couldn't walk for three days. Finally, flying a hang-glider for 'Sensation' ended with him crash-landing in a patch of thorns.

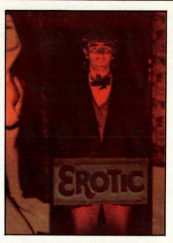

Most of the 1,500 extras in the 'Pinball Wizard' sequence were students from the local technical college. In part-payment to them, and for many of the other extras, The Who gave a private concert in Portsmouth. This came just four days after The Who had played to nearly 100,000 fans at the much publicised and televised Charlton Festival. The Portsmouth concert (above and left) was a totally different affair; no publicity, no press, no police. Also, it was much better. Townshend said, "It's one of the best gigs we've done." For most of the blind and disabled extras it was their first experience of a live pop-concert. Most of them enjoyed it, but found it 'a bit bewildering.' Afterwards one extra who was blind, her ears still ringing, jokingly accused The Who of trying to deafen her as well.

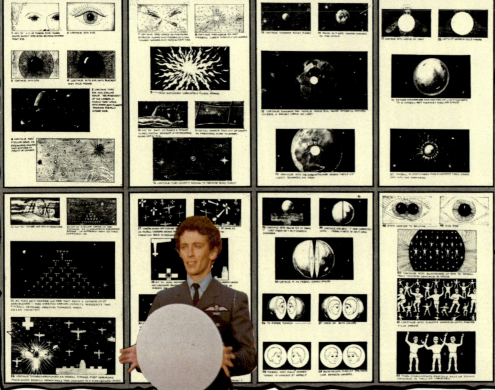
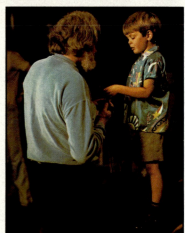

When Tommy first becomes deaf, dumb and blind, his parents try to make amends for their crime by lavishing affection on him. They take him to the funfair, but instead of experiencing the fair, Tommy is taken on an inner journey by his mind. 'The Amazing Journey' is a profound, mystical and open-ended song: The perfect tool for Russell's brand of film making, where he can indulge himself in a bit of visual extravaganza. A look at his interview, later in the book, reveals that the ingredients in this visual cocktail – RAF and Catholic church symbols – are quite clearly drawn from his past. The original storyboard (left) shows Russell's penchant for fantasy.

(Top right) Young Tommy played by Barry Winch talks to Russell while filming the dancing scene (top). Hundreds of small images of Tommy dancing in space, were put together to fill the screen. (Right) "What a way to spend Easter." Captain Walker, played by Robert Powell on a cross in the form of a wartime bomber, having his trousers repaired and (below left and below) himself prepared. Images of his father appear throughout Tommy's amazing journey. Another bit of Russell symbolism with Captain Walker being set up (left) on top of a mountain.

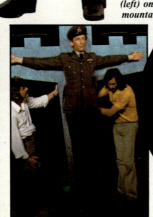
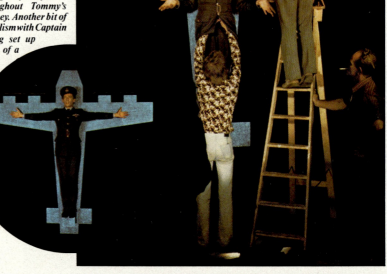

Filming on fairground rides required a lot of skill and patience. Much of the footage for 'The Amazing Journey' could not be used as it was jerky and blurred. The difficult task of trying to keep a hand-held camera firm while being thrown around at high speed, was that of camera operator Ronnie Taylor. Seen (left) on the fast 'Speedway' ride as Oliver Reed and Ken Russell look on, and being steadied on the 'Carousel' (below). Tommy and his mum ride on the 'Kiddies Choo-Choo' (above). His 'amazing journey' takes Tommy in a wartime bomber with his father (above right). Tommy's trip starts when Frank tries to make him play on a machine that fires on aeroplanes (right). Getting the 'effect' of aeroplane-like crosses in space, was a real cliff hanger. Russell was not satisfied and rejected it. It was then re-made, but completed so late that it was nearly left out. But it seems worth the trouble as it is such an exciting visual effect.

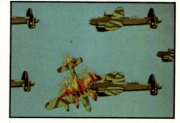

There's a man I've found
Could bring us all joy!
There's a doctor I've found can cure the boy
A doctor I've found
Can cure the boy!

There's a man I've found
Could remove his sorrow
He lives in this town,
Let's see him tomorrow

Let's see him tomorrow

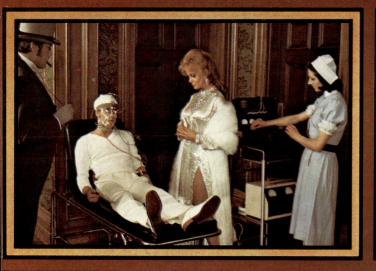

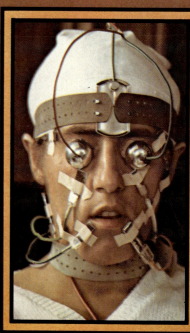

He seems to be completely unreceptive
The tests I gave him showed no sense at all
His eyes react to light, the dials detect it
He hears but cannot answer to your call

*See me, feel me, touch me, heal me
See me, feel me, touch me, heal me*

There is no chance, no untried operation
All hope lies with him and none with me
Imagine though the shock from isolation
When he suddenly can hear and speak and see

*See me, feel me, touch me, heal me
See me, feel me, touch me, heal me*

His eyes can see
His ears can hear, his lips speak,
All the time the needles flick and rock
No machine can give the kind of stimulation
Needed to remove his inner block

I often wonder what it is he's feeling
Has he ever heard a word I've said
Look at him now in the mirror dreaming
What is happening in his head?

What is happening in his head?
I wish I knew, I wish I knew

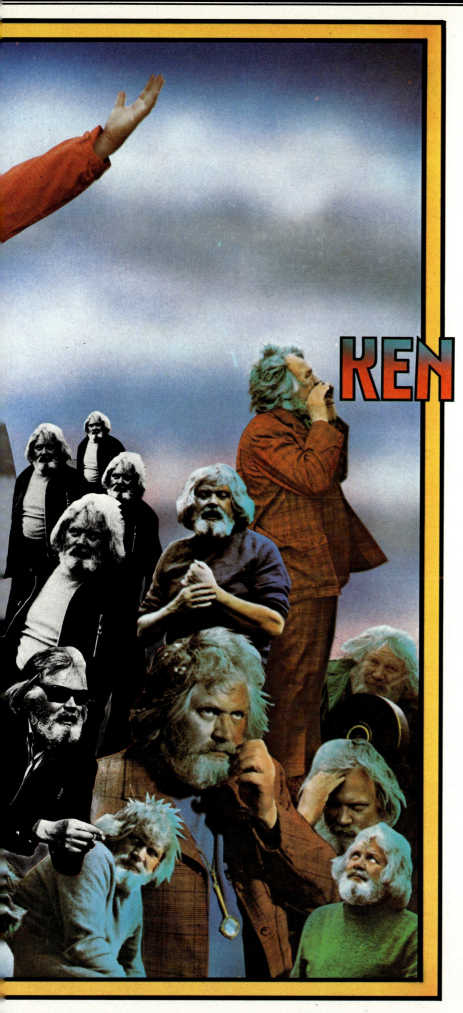

Through all the various projects and false starts in turning 'Tommy' from the original 'rock opera' into a film, Ken Russell was always the Who's first choice as director. Russell's life has included working as a merchant seaman, an electrician in the RAF, an assistant in an art gallery and a photographer. His first involvement in cinema was passive: "It was just something different, something outside one's own reality, and one just dreamed along with it. I was never particularly interested in the technique of film making, of how things were done".

Music was what first inspired him to make films, and he still says he'd rather have been a composer than a film director. His first films were low-budget, amateur productions, and his first real success as a film-maker was with the BBC, working on the arts programme 'Monitor'. Among his subjects there were Prokoviev, Elgar, Bartok, Debussy, Delius and Richard Strauss. While with the BBC he took time off to make two feature films—a comedy called 'French Dressing' in 1963 and the third in a series of Len Deighton spy thrillers 'Billion Dollar Brain' which starred Michael Caine as Harry Palmer.

KEN RUSSELL

But it was his film of D. H. Lawrence's 'Women In Love' which established him as a cinema director. He followed that with 'The Music Lovers' about the life of Tchaikovsky, 'The Devils', 'The Boyfriend', the musical starring Twiggy, 'Savage Messiah', 'Mahler' and 'Tommy'.

Russell says that 'Tommy' was first brought to his attention by Tony Palmer, who was working with him as an assistant producer at the BBC. He got the record, liked the music but "couldn't make any sense of the story". It was three years later that he finally agreed to do the film: "although I had another project in hand at the time, about Gargantua, the man with the biggest prick in the world". He went to see Lou Reisner's stage production—"a farce, the worst performance I had seen of something so good in my life"—which didn't give him any more clues as to the story, and he decided to write his own screenplay: "I got Pete to give me every piece of literature he had about it, and I read through a pile a mile high. I pointed out there would need to be some more songs to clarify the story. It never occurred to me to use dialogue".

The following interview with Ken Russell is by David Litchfield and it originally appeared in *The Image* magazine.

What percentage of films that you start actually see the light of day?

Reasonably high, although there's one script, it was called 'The Angels', I could never get off the ground. I kept trying, and I gradually sort of pirated it as I've gone along and I get bits of it into most of my films; there's a bit of it in 'Tommy', there's a bit in 'Mahler'. Oh, there is also another thing that I wrote, adapted rather, from some stories by Isaac Babel. He's the best revolutionary writer, he wrote during the revolution in Russia, his stories were so ambiguous, I mean they were straightforward but they could never quite work out whose side he was on so they shot him. I find now that I really want to write all the scripts myself.

But have you done a lot of writing in the past?

No, not at all really, it just evolved out of necessity. I've generally worked on scripts with friends whose work I've known and who have been very symphatic towards shared ideas. John McGrath wrote quite a number of screen plays but now he's gone off with his theatre. Melvyn Bragg, who I worked with at the BBC, wrote the Debussy film, the Rousseau film and 'The Music Lovers', And then I started.

Do you like bringing all the people together or in an ideal situation would you do the whole thing on your own?

Well, I suppose that's the ideal thing. I'd certainly like to dub the film myself, but you can't actually. I operate the camera quite a bit—there's quite a bit of my camera at work in Mahler. I advise on the lighting, say what I want, what effect I want, I know exactly because I was a photographer you see, and I also made three films, shot them myself, before I joined the BBC, so I know a bit about it. I like getting actors around me who are very symphatetic to our mode of working which is fast and mobile. We shot 'Mahler' in about seven weeks, which was pretty good going. I tend to have a team of actors I use, not all the time. I always try and work with the same people I like. The editor I have worked with and who has always cut my films, is Mike Bradsell, although he's now doing 'Stardust' which will clash and so I'm using his protege, Stuart Baird. He's been Mike's assistant for years and I have known him since he was a runner on 'Women In Love'. I've worked with the same couple of producers. I sort of alternate between Roy Baird and Harry Benn, and my wife does all the costumes so it's really a tight-knit group.

You make it sound as if you sort of churn them out.

Well I do churn them out. You just simply repeat the process with variations, but having said that, each film is entirely different. It really is an odyssey on which you have adventures on the way.

The point about choosing a composer like Mahler is that his music deals with the eternal question of love, death, life after death, eternity—imponderable sort of things which I like to explore and find out for myself and try to answer questions that we all want to know—and I find that if you can get on to this peculiar sort of hypnotic mystical wavelength which is music, which is this intangible thing . . . I mean it is the most mysterious invention of man to actually conjure incredible sounds out of the air. If one gets on to that wavelength and explores paths that the music is about, I find that I certainly get some insight into the questions.

Do you ever get to the stage where you get slightly shattered by the individual?

Oh, that's the excitement of it. I mean it's like a detective story, you're given the clues and certain bits of evidence, which is the music. I'm suspicious of facts because nobody really knows all the facts. So a book on a composer which just gives you the facts of his life is very useful up to a point, but you've really got to listen to the music. The music tells you if he's lying.

A case in point is Tchaikovsky, I mean Moldesty's brother burnt all his diaries when he died and this meant that he saw ones that were dealing with homosexuality, for instance, and there was a big cover up job and so on and so forth. But even in Russia today they don't admit he was a homosexual. It doesn't really matter; the fact is that they just think he's a benign old country gentleman sitting there in a rocking chair, and wrote these schizophrenic symphonies and they fail to equate the two. Then when Melvyn and I assimilated the facts and started working out the script we found, for instance there was one scene which he did document about his abortive honeymoon which he spent on an express train with this girl Nina and he said he just got her drunk and sat up all night. Well we wrote a little scene, at least Mervyn wrote the scene, and then I thought we don't need words here. I mean the music must express the drama. Given these two facts we re-enacted the scene by getting in this very small compartment which we built and put on rubber tyres for rocking and she (Glenda Jackson) just undressed and he (Richard Chamberlain) was in the corner. We rocked it and I played this music as loud as I possibly could, blaring out on the loud speakers, and it just seemed to happen before our eyes. One finds out, maybe it was like that, maybe it wasn't but the point is when you actually do build up an atmosphere I find that it doesn't have the absolute factual reality but has a reality of its own that's very close. It doesn't always work but when it does you just feel it, everyone gets excited and surprised, and that's also why I like making films.

Do you think about the film's commercial potential while you're constructing it?

No. Well I don't really think about it, I think that if it interests me there's a chance that it might interest other people. I simply work on that thesis.

Who do you think are the modern equivalents of the type of people that you make films about?

Well I would say very probably pop people. I wouldn't have said it before I

Russell is the kind of director who works more with the camera than with the actors. Although he brings good performances out of his actors, it is his visual imagery that is most outstanding. Experienced actors like Jack Nicholson and Ann-Margret (top left) can be left to 'get on with it,' whereas both Keith Moon (top right) and Eric Clapton (above left) need more guidance and direction. Whether in his 'directors chair' (above) or 'putting the boot in' with Ann-Margret and Roger Daltrey (left), his involvement is total. (Below) With Barry Winch after filming at the funfair. (Far left) The deep thinker and the flowery gesticulator.

Tommy can you hear me?
Can I help to cheer you?
Tommy can you hear me?
Can you feel me near you?
Oh Tommy, Tommy
Tommy...

Tommy can you hear me?
Can you feel me near you?
Tommy can you see me?
Can I help to cheer you?
Oh Tommy, Tommy,
Tommy,
Tommy, Tommy, Tommy,
Tommy, Tommy,
Tommy...

TOMMY CAN YOU HEAR ME?

SMASH THE MIRROR!

You don't answer my call
With even a nod or a twitch
But you gaze at your
own reflection!
You don't seem to see me
But I think you can see yourself
How can the mirror affect you?

Can you hear me?
Or do I surmise
That you fear me?
Can you feel my temper
RISE, RISE, RISE,
RISE, RISE, RISE,
RISE, RISE, RISE,
RISE, RISE, RISE, RISE…

Do you hear or fear or
Do I smash the mirror?
Do you hear or fear or
Do I smash the mirror?

started work on Tommy because I didn't know enough about them, I'd never met any, I'd read about them of course and I suppose if I'd thought about it a bit I would have still have said that but I mean it's very forcibly brought home to me, having worked with Pete Townshend, Keith Moon, John Entwistle and Roger Daltrey who are all totally different type characters, and yet there is this entity. They've got a strange sort of discipline which isn't like any discipline I've ever known.

The first time I went into the recording studios someone was six hours late and I sort of got very impatient and I phoned Townshend up the next day and said I was very upset this person didn't turn up and, you know, any other director would have walked out for good. He said: "I'm sorry, he's like that". And then I realised that obviously they had been waiting for this chap on and off for eight years and he's always been six hours late. Townshend said: "well he sometimes might be five hours late, and sometimes actually, once in a blue moon, might come on time". I realised that there are different sets of values and disciplines, if it works for them being six hours late and instead of working normal hours recording, if they work from midnight till six in the morning, that's their way of doing it and at the same time they are very sort of committed people to their work. They've got a sort of strangeness once they do start working, they're very talented and very dedicated. It just took me quite a bit to re-orientate my own set, rather old-fashioned ways with the way they think, and it's quite a revitalising process.

Do you write music yourself?

No, I'd like to, I like to become involved. I mean, since I have been working with Townshend I've suggested certain things, the development of certain tunes that he's already got for instrumental passages which appear with visual things happening around them.

Do you work on more than one project at a time?

I might do. While I've been working on Tommy I've been writing 'Gershwin' and 'Liszt' and finishing off 'Mahler', but I like working like that because it's a good excuse to sit down for hours playing endless music, and I find that the music itself does give me amazing ideas.

Do you ever stop thinking about film?

No, I don't really, I never do. The thing is that when we are researching a film you read about kindred things. When I'm not actually filming I don't go to the cinema at all unless I have to. I like going to the theatre occasionally in great spates, after making a film or after dubbing it a lot when you see it on the screen, because you get so sick of the ever-flickering image that you want some flesh and blood to look at in the way of entertainment.

When you're making a film though, isn't it rather like a theatre to you?

Oh yes it is then of course, that's the most exciting thing, much more exciting than theatre because I've never done anything for the stage and I find it rather terrifying because the scenes I hate doing most are scenes in films where people sit around a table eating a meal. That's my nightmare. Specifically it used to be that I could put down half a dozen directors whose work influenced me image-wise, and then I feel now I have assimilated them and do my own brand of imagery but we all have to start . . .

What influences you visually?

Well there are certain things Sometimes I deliberately look at paintings before I go to sleep, certainly the Belgian chap, the surrealist who's just dead, does loads of bread floating about the sky and trains coming through fireplaces, and other books and pictures. I look at them before I go to sleep and I think that is your mind's most impressionable time. Although I don't use those images as such, I like to think that maybe they trigger off other images, so that when I do come to write a script I've got plenty of strange things in my head, floating around, which I can draw on. I went to an exhibition the other day of Edvard Munch's work and maybe if I'd have shot 'Mahler' after I'd been to that it would have looked a bit different because that exhibition made more impression on me, I think, than any other painting I've probably ever seen.

It worked on two levels which I always like doing, I mean, there's the level of the picture itself and there's the subconscious effect it has on you, you don't quite know why. It's to do with the shape and also the content. The trouble with film is that it's O.K. for Picasso to do a cubist type portrait of Brigitte Bardot, but it's not O.K. for a director to take liberties as it were with, or put their own interpretation on a character who has lived, and I've often been criticised for that. It's because they don't look beneath the surface and look at the shape of the image. 'Mahler' is full of symbolic things all the way through because in a film that's only 100 minutes long you've got to make everything work. Every dress for instance, has a

Russell and Robert Powell film a close-up in a Lancaster bomber's cockpit for the film's first song; 'Captain Walker.' Flames by courtesy of bottled gas.

symbolic meaning. A lot of people think I'm quite wilful and do things just for the fun or just out of sheer cussedness but actually it's all quite calculated on the psychological effect. So in nearly all my films, especially in 'Mahler', everything works on two levels at once and whether the audience knows that or doesn't know it is beside the point. That is why I think some of my films worry people and they can't think quite why. In a hundred minutes I just give an impression of the person as he strikes me that is all—given the facts, given the music, given all the things and letting them all just wash through your head and out into a film. You know it's a feeling of the person I want to get, not the correct positioning of his third shirt button.

Do your films make money?

The only film that's gone into profit that I've made that's been admitted, I mean they send you a lot of figures, but when they say that the advertising on 'The Boyfriend' cost $6 million, it's going to take a long time to make any money you see, and how can you prove it didn't without actually going there and asking to see their books and so on and so forth? So the only film they admitted has made a profit was 'Women In Love', and then you get a few hundred pounds every so often in excess of your fee as a director.

There's a lot of friction between the money and the creation?

Well, there usually is, but a very good example of there not being is 'Mahler'. I think David Puttnam is one of the best producers we've got. He got the money from one source or another and didn't interfere at all with the film and the cutting of it or anything, and was as generally helpful as he could be. The thing is that when you are dealing with the Americans, and this is about the first film that hasn't been sponsored by the Americans, when your film leaves your hands, unless you're someone like Kubrick who can do what he wants, you can't stop them cutting it and ruining it. 'The Devils', for example: it was pretty good in those days, four or five years ago, they allowed everything in although they kept saying cut out those shots of Oliver having his legs crushed and they said there was too much blood, and in the end I said "do you know how much blood there is in that sequence?" They said "well, there's too much", and I said "12 frames, which is half a second". The thing doesn't have to go on a long time to make an impact. It was only in their minds, rather like when Alexander Walker said "We see vivid scenes of Oliver Reed having his testicles crushed" —that was probably wishful thinking on his part because there is no such thing, and he argued on television that it was there.

That's something about your film-making, you pack so much into the thing?

Yes, that's how I like to do it. It's brain impact, it's brain packing, I don't know. I mean things do happen enormously fast anyway. If you're driving along in a car, you probably notice sometimes you're looking out of the window if you're being driven and you pass maybe an alleyway or a gateway between brick walls and you see someone in the act of doing something either getting on a bicycle or throwing a ball or whatever and you could only see that image if you're travelling at 60 m.p.h. for I suppose about 1/500th of a second. Well, you've seen it and you know it and it's very, very clear and I think films should be the same. It's nothing to do with the quality of the film, whether it's a good or a bad film, it's just a physical thing I think and so you've got to pack everything into those two hours.

I think that 'Mahler', for instance, is probably the best film I've done on an artist, because he was a very interesting man. It's probably not as entertaining as the Isadora Duncan film which was only 50 minutes and really had to be packed, crammed, and it contained more information than any film I've ever made but I hope put across in an entertaining manner.

With 'Tommy' I've had much more control because, as I say, it's been done with an English group instead of American, and the original opera is very good, I think, but there were various gaps missing so far as the film would be concerned. It just starts with a murder, you know nothing about the people at all and with the film you've really got to associate or be involved with the people involved in the situation to arouse the audience's interest, so we've tacked on a beginning which shows who the characters are and what their life is and so forth. It's very condensed, it only lasts about five or ten minutes, but it says quite a lot about them and Pete's also written four or five new songs which I felt were necessary again to build up the characters or make the plot clearer. But having said that, there is no speaking in the film, it's all

singing and it's all music, and it's a challenge and I think it sets out to . . . I mean it deals with a pretty big thing, false Messiahs, true Messiahs, man being God, God being man, whatever. That's what interests me. It's a recurring theme in my films. I mean, all my films are very Catholic, but people never mention it.

Do you think this was because of your spiritual development while becoming involved in Catholicism rather than Catholicism itself?

Yes, that's it, that's it, yes. I think one of the reasons I left it was that I couldn't live up to it, I mean I wasn't good enough to continue and I also didn't believe in a lot of it, the more I thought about it.

What sort of education did you have?

Well none at all to speak of. I went to a succession of nondescript schools, local schools in Southampton, and then I went away to the Nautical College at Pangbourne where I didn't learn much about tying knots but I did learn a bit about putting on shows. We used to have an end of term concert and they used to always dress up in grey flannels with a white shirt and cap singing 'The Fishermen Of England Are Working At Their Nets'. I changed all that, I got them all in drag and dressed them up as Carmen Miranda singing 'South American Way'. That was all the rage in the 1940's. I used to break bounds to go and see all the Hollywood musicals of the time, or the Betty Grable pin up girl, and I was very impressed by the star-studded musicals like 'Star Spangled Banner' and 'Stage Door Canteen'.

They made a great impression on me, those films, and then I knew I wanted to make films. I started making my first one at the college in my last term. I never saw it but it lasted about three minutes or less.

So you never became a naval officer in fact?

Well, I was at sea for one trip, that was enough—I was Sixth Officer-cum-Apprentice on a boat that went to Australia and New Zealand. We had rather a strange captain. He used to make you stand on the spot, can you imagine standing on the spot for four hours in the tropical sun, the ship just rising gently up and down on an endless swell? However I like the atmosphere of the sea and I like things involved with water. The elements, they play a big part in all my films. 'Mahler' is full of water and fire. I haven't got any snow in this one.

What happened after you left the sea?

I was very poor for a very long time and struggled along and taught photography at technical college for £3.10s a week and it was bloody hard. I suppose the worst period of my life was before that when I came out of the Air Force. I knew that I wanted to make films then, I just simply knew I had to make them, and I went to all the film studios there were, but they all turned me down. It was a closed shop. I had my terrible demob suit from the Air Force, and in those days in British Films you really had to be in the know and I was being turned away from those doors and my gratuity was running out. I came to the point when I thought well, I've got to get a job. I'm not going to get into films, I've got to get a job and I looked in some papers and I saw . . . I think it was for a carpenter. I was quite good at woodwork, and I went along to this factory and I just stood at the entrance. I saw this clock and I saw the people clocking in, and I thought I'll starve rather than do that, so then I went home and I looked up all these art galleries they used to advertise on the Underground, of all the shows on in London and I had a vague feeling that I, I didn't know anything about painting, but I thought, well, there might be more in this, even though the pay wasn't going to be so good as working in the furniture factory. So I wrote to all the galleries and three replied. One was the National Gallery, and I went round to that. I met this curator, I suppose he was, and he says "you're too young". I said I was in my early twenties. He said "well you don't want to become like these", and there were all these men in blue suits, with uniforms, asleep in chairs, nodding off, and I said "No, I don't suppose I do".

The last one, called the Lefevre Galleries, was in Bond Street, I thought well I'm jolly

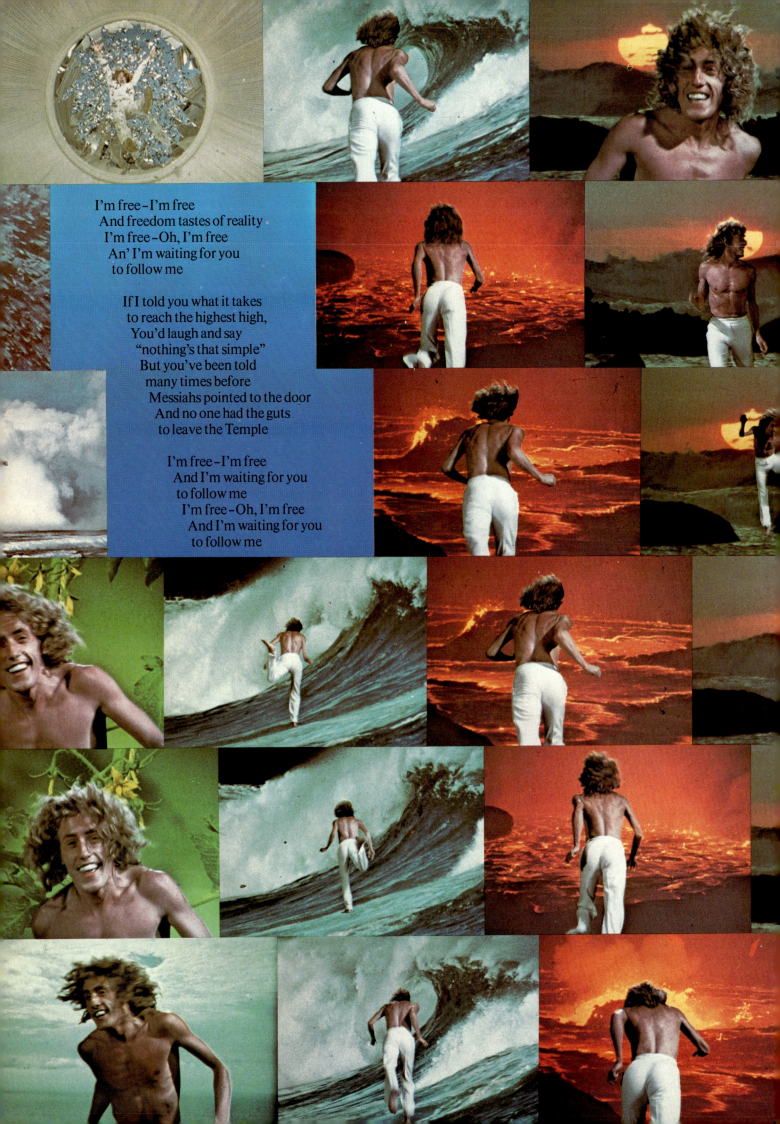

well going to get in there so I went along and I . . . the day before the interview I looked at all the pictures on the wall and they were by someone called Sickert, I'd never heard of, I didn't like them, they were all brown, but I went back and I went to the library that night and I read all about Sickert and I went back for the job the next day, and I met the owner, and I said "Ah yes, Camden Town period, very interesting, that was, what, 1891?, yes probably one of his greatest portraits", and he was very impressed. So I got the job in the art gallery at £3.10s. and I guess I began to start looking at things very clearly because I had all day to do nothing but look at the paintings. I left after about six months to take up ballet because I thought I might have a go at that—I'd met someone in the Air Force who was a ballet dancer. I just knew I didn't want to be a carpenter or work in my father's boot shop. I just knew I didn't want to do that. I tried as I say, ballet and photography and so forth.

They're all useful because I've learned about movement, I've learned about images. When you see no possible way out, you know you have some of this mythical dream that one day you're going to make it or whatever, but then you begin to think no, no, I'm not and I'm sick of it, living on porridge. I used to live on porridge for years, and it's not, as I say, that one's uncomfortable, it's just there's no hope of changing your existence. That's the worst thing.

What age do you think you began to get a grip of yourself properly?

I think when I became a Catholic, I was about 28, quite late really. I was too sentimental and nostalgic—I still am, I suppose, but I now know I am and I know how to combat it. I know not to fall into the trap and I understand when I'm getting too ridiculous. At the time there didn't seem any way out then suddenly, it suddenly clicked, like a light going on. I suddenly saw I could make it work. I started to make a reasonable living as a cameraman, stills photographer, it wasn't great but I struggled along. Some days, some weeks you didn't do much and some you did, but then I started making these amateur films. Of course, I thought everyone was a masterpiece and would immediately be recognised

as such and I'd be given carte blanche to direct any film that came along. I was a bit disillusioned but at least when you know you're on the way, that gives you great heart. You can take off, and put up with anything then.

Do you day-dream a lot?

Yes, all the time, but productively. I dream with a purpose, I just don't go off into sort of vague miasmic drifting. The only trouble is you find that so many things are going on at once in your head that they have to come out.

And when did you get married?

I'm 46 now, or 7, born in 1927. I've been married about 17 years. I guess . . . 28 I think.

So that happened also . . .

Yes, I became a Catholic and got married shortly after that.

Your first films were flops; how did you manage to get another chance?

You see I was very lucky because I only came out of the B.B.C. to make them and I went back immediately and carried on, so that was O.K. I was quite fortunate.

Are there any individual films, other people's films, that still astonish you?

Well I never get tired of seeing 'Citizen Kane'. I got tired of Eisenstein, I don't like him any more. I used to think he was the best, but now I don't like him at all. Very operatic, pretentious, obvious propaganda. I'm a great propagandist myself, in things I believe in, but I don't believe in necessarily ramming it down people's throats in such an obvious way. I think more subtlety is required and I don't think his films are subtle enough. I enjoy the spectacle of them, all these galloping horses over the ice and so forth but really they don't wear very well. Take something like the Jean Vigo films, again I could see them forever, those three films he did. Those and early German expressionist films, I still like seeing them and also Hollywood musicals.

John Schlesinger does four or five films in a night sometimes. He suddenly decides he's going to see them so he rushes round and does ten minutes in each cinema just to see what's happening.

I could almost appreciate that. I wouldn't mind . . . yes, that sounds a good idea.

When you're working on someone like Mahler, does he become almost an inanimate object which you can move round?

I'm not sure, the film changes as you go along. Every film has a particular quality of its own and you go along with it. You can't really fight what you're getting, well you can but I think you're a fool if you do. You just go along, which is why I can't understand certain directors who will sit in a chair with a camera crew of a hundred round them waiting for a particular cloud formation. We know who they are, or who he is, and to me that's insanity because I think films are like happenings and I love being at the mercy of the elements. A lot of my films take place outside. I don't like working in the studio that much. I like getting outside as much as possible. I like finding locations by chance, the sudden possibility that you might be drenched or you've to use what's at hand, that's terrifically exciting.

Do you find that's sometimes difficult to get over to the technicians?

No, I'm generally pretty lucky with the conditions that I get, I wouldn't probably be sitting about anyway. But for instance in 'Mahler', when we wanted a storm, a storm came and it lasted for three days which is how long it took us to shoot the film and then it stopped and I wanted a brilliant sun sequence and the sun came out and we shot the summer sequence. In the storm I had two cameras going, everyone was rushing around. My wife was directing one scene, we had the assistant director throwing leaves in the air . . . I love getting everyone at it so that all their inhibitions go, and they are all enjoying the happening.

Do you think every film director, not only directors of films but anybody that's connected with films and making them, has to be a bit omnipotent, whether you like it or not, even if you're not feeling omnipotent, you've got to be up there to sort of create this excitement so that things do happen?

Of course you have, I mean, unless you are they won't get excited and they won't do it. If you're not excited and you're the one in charge, how can you expect them to be?

Did you find in making 'Tommy' that there is any spiritual conflict between you and Peter and did you research him?

No, I could make it a story of his beliefs, I find they are very similar to mine. He likes to be involved in . . . Meher Baba. I am involved in my own beliefs and obviously in itself they are the same thing. It's about the same subject and everybody has their own individual approach to it and obviously it works and he gets something out of his spiritual goal or vision . . . and I do out of mine. I don't think that they are that different because I have talked to him at great lengths about this. I mean, before I started writing the screen-play I appreciated exactly what it was to him and that it was a spiritual piece, I didn't want to impose my own ideas and so I asked him precisely what he meant by each piece. I believe that people don't know why they do things, I think that an instinctive artist like Pete Townshend doesn't necessarily have to explain why he wrote or what it means exactly and I think the trouble with the 20th century is that people want to try and explain things too much. They like explanations and so there were certain areas where I just sensed that I knew what he meant so I suggested this in the script. The first one I did a very long treatment before I wrote it then he said, "yes that's right, yes that's right". I think there was only one thing that he disagreed with, then I wrote the script and there is nothing he disagrees with in that. Yes, I researched everything about Townshend all he had ever said about Tommy and of his beliefs and read about these things before I attempted it so I did the same sort of research but on him. I mean I haven't thought of that consciously until now, that is what I obviously did.

Did you listen to 'Quadrophenia'?

Yes.

What did you think of it?

Well I haven't really heard enough to say. I would have to hear it several times. It doesn't mean as much to me, it doesn't excite me as much as 'Tommy' because I am not au fait with the mods, although I liked it a lot when I was there during the recording. Again it's this adventure thing, it's this chance thing, this luck thing. We were there the night they recorded a number called 'Rain' and there was a cloudburst and they wanted a stereo rain effect. We were in this caravan outside and bit by bit the playing stopped except for the piano and I went in and the floor and the roof had caved in as they were singing and the rain had really deluged them. They were soaking wet and there were firemen with a hose pumping it out except for the actual man in the cubicle playing the piano and he was gamely playing on and he was up to his neck in water and when they opened the door it poured like a waterfall, which was very funny.

You seem to be the type of character who is quite capable of having Jungian type experiences of grandiose proportions, I don't mean put on, something like that happening and the whole thing assuming incredible meaning.

Yes I think I am probably given to that. I think that's what films probably are to me, I mean you are given a sentence and it has to take on a bigger proportion.

In a way films are a sort of indulgence. Do you ever get any guilt about it?

Oh no, none at all.

Or do you just love it and thank God it happened?

Exactly, I mean I don't want to be a film director I would rather be a composer. I'm quite content to be a film director, but if I was given the chance of giving it up, if some magical person came along and said well, you can now from this moment on when I click my fingers know as much about the technique of writing music and playing the piano as you know about films, yeah, I would change like that.

What stops you from sitting down and doing the hard work and learning?

Well I haven't time to do it, I mean I would have to stop making films and I would probably be very mediocre as a composer. I could learn the technique of composing but as I'm not meant to be one, I'd probably write rubbish. I've no idea, I have no tunes in my head, but I would rather do that, to me that's got many more possibilities than film-making. Of course you've got the performers who play the work whether it's rock beat or classical beat, but you don't really rely on them, I mean it is there and it's what you've written that matters . . . like writing is there and nobody can say it isn't but if it's a bad performance it's a bad performance. With a film you are at the mercy of about 80 people, if it's a bad film it's still tough. I could read the script of 'Mahler' before I shot it and imagine it all in my head and that's the most exciting bit for me when I've finished the script and I've got it all there. It's then you have to go through the boring process of making it. But then when you start looking for locations and start meeting actors, then it gets interesting again and I like looking for locations perhaps more than anything, because it's an excuse to go off again and discover England. It would be lovely if the script I've written of 'Gershwin' didn't have to be made. I can see it all, why should I go and bloody well make it?

Well that's the thing, why is it boring?

Well why is it boring . . .

Why don't you just write a book?

Well . . . because I'm not setting myself up as a novelist.

Couldn't you get down what you wanted?

No, no no, because that's the trouble when people read my scripts they can't make them out. They say, yeah, this is very short, there's no characterisation in it. They said that with the 'Devils'—65 pages, this is a feature film it's only going to last 15 minutes. I said it's going to last 2 hours and it very likely lasted over two hours. I said well, I'm not a novelist, you know, if you want a novel written instead of a screen play get someone else. The same thing happened with 'Mahler', the British Film Finance saw the script and that was 65 pages and they said this can't be a feature film and its two hours long, they couldn't see it lasting two hours but I knew it would. My scripts are really shorthand which I discuss in great detail, and the actors and everyone get involved in it. As far as a shooting script is concerned that is what we'll always shoot, I don't change it too much, I mean I take advantage of anything that might happen and I always take ideas from anyone, if someone comes up with a good idea I'll use it, even from the clapper boy. The script really is like a cartoon as opposed to a painting, it's a rough, the dialogue is there and the instructions and that's about it.

Are you very conscious of time?

You see I've got this thing that I have to get as much done as possible in a very short time, you know I might be knocked over tomorrow—I'm not going to live forever. Then I've got so much to do that I want to do, I just want to do it, that's the important thing you know before I die I'd like to make 20 more films, I doubt if I will, I doubt it very much indeed and then I may not want to make them anymore but for the moment I want to keep churning out films and get them out of the way. I mean it's almost like getting the ideas out of your head.

It's almost like an incredible form of analysis, isn't it?

Oh yes, it is, I mean in 'Mahler', although it's a film about Mahler it's also about me, but he's a Cancer, he was born at the beginning of July. I was as well and I think I can understand him. I think I can see lots of my faults in him. I mean his hang-ups are my hang-ups, when he carries on I carry on. The fact that he is a composer and I am a film director is rather immaterial as I say, I'm interested in the things he's interested in. I suppose in every film one does a different part of one's personality comes out.

Does it attract you to go back and work for T.V.?

The B.B.C. want me to, but they plan so far ahead it's very difficult to work it out. I mean I've been going to do a film with them for donkey's ages, they say can you do it, say September 1975 you know and I don't know if I can or not. I don't know what I'll be doing. It's too far away, it's gradually got like that. The good thing about working on Monitor was that you go up to Hugh Weldon and say let's make a film on Bartok, he would say, tell me about Bartok . . . how are you going to do it . . . right, go and do it. Today, you can't do that. I wanted to do a film on Vaughan Williams for B.B.C. They griped about the budget so I saw John Colshaw but finally they said no and so on and so forth but they gradually came up with the money and then it was too late and then they said well we can't make it until 1976 or something ridiculous like that. They've got too big and they just have to plan so far ahead. I don't know why they do it, but it makes it very hard for any outside film director to plan anything. The chap who does it best is Jack Gold who does very good films for the drama department and at the same time makes feature films.

So you think to some extent the B.B.C. is no longer the rich place for learning the business that it was?

No, I think it is a very good place for learning the business. I think we were particularly lucky in that we were given sort of more or less carte blanche to do as we liked. Bearing in mind we were always told, what I have always thought was my best lesson, that because we were dealing with artists we mustn't be arty ourselves or make arty films. They should be entertaining films and that's the best lesson we ever learned— to package the information and entertainment into a rather attractive parcel. And I gradually learned that as we followed the main feature film on Sunday night when anyone saw Monitor, the average viewer would take x number of seconds to get up and turn it off, so if I had a film on we would drop the logo thing at the beginning and put it at the end and I would devise an opening sequence for my films which would stop them turning off. You remember how I started it the 'Debussy' film—a naked girl is tied to a post and she is being slowly shot full of arrows . . . well they are not going to turn it off quite as quickly as if I had shown a more conventional opening.

SENSATION

You'll feel me coming
A new vibration
From afar you'll see me
I'm a sensation!
I'm a sensation!

I overwhelm as I approach you
Make your lungs hold breath inside!
Grounded angels your wings are broken
Time to mend and learn to fly

They worship me and all I touch
Hazy eyed they catch my glance
Pleasant shudders shake their senses
My warm momentum throws their stance

You'll feel me coming
A new vibration
From afar you'll see me
I'm a sensation!
I'm a sensation!

Soon you'll see me, can't you feel me?
I'm coming!
Send your troubles dancing
I know the answer
I'm coming
I'm coming . . .
I'm a sensation!

You'll feel me coming
A new vibration
From afar you'll see me
I'm a sensation!
I'm a sensation!

I leave a trail of rooted people
Mesmerised by just the sight
The few I touched now are disciples
Love as One, I am the Light . . .
I am the Light

To so many people, and certainly to people who know The Who, Roger Daltrey *is* Tommy. Obviously, he played the part when The Who did it on stage, and he even took part in Lou Reisner's stage production. Pete Townshend felt he'd been lumbered enough: when a production of 'Tommy' was staged on Broadway, they even dressed up the guy in a fringed jacket to look like the well-worn publicity photographs of Daltrey. For that reason, Townshend was against Daltrey taking the part in the film to begin with. "But Ken made me realise that to everyone else he was Tommy—he was the right man with the right voice".

Russell possibly had other reservations to begin with: like could he act? But the first day's filming brought Daltrey a baptism of fire (and water and plenty more) as an actor, after which he felt happier about doing it. And Russell decided that he'd do. "Roger is a revelation," he told the film company publicist, "he's incredible, a natural, a brilliant performer. He's the only Tommy". Russell was impressed enough to want him as Liszt in his next picture, Ollie Reed reckons he could be the first singer properly to make the transition to films since Frank Sinatra, and Townshend says he surprised everyone by being as good as he was in a difficult part.

Roger Daltrey has ways of avoiding a stigma: "I'm not a film star. The Who is definitely my first love", he told the English music paper *Sounds*. "I'm only doing the Liszt film because Tommy is painted with such a white brush, and dear old Franz will change all that—out comes the blue paint for Franz, that'll put the image back where it belongs. If I never do another film I don't want people to say it's because I'm Tommy, 'cause I bloody ain't".

He was dubious about doing 'Tommy' at first too: "I was worried about the whole concept of a film with pop stars in it—we tend to have an inbuilt image that can do a lot of damage when you need people to identify with a character. But there was slightly less of a problem with me because so many people, having seen me do the stage show, tend to relate my face to Tommy. Really though, I never felt I'd got the part until I'd completed the first day on the set and Ken seemed satisfied—I thought if someone of his experience wasn't worried then it shouldn't worry me". The first day was the Cousin Kevin sequence where he got dragged around by the hair, dumped in a bath of evil smelling liquid, drenched by a high-pressure fire hose and dried out with an electric iron. So he earned his wings. As it happened, that first day began to look like child's play as the film progressed. He used a stunt man only once, in a scene which involved a jump from a high tower: "The real problem was we couldn't find anyone who looked enough like me. I think you can tell it isn't me in that scene, but we had to do it because it was really dangerous".

That jump involved a kite, but Daltrey had his fun on that machine in another scene. "We were filming in the Lake District and I had to go right up on the top of this huge hill and perch there till take-off. We had to wait for a bit of sun to come out, and suddenly along comes this fucking great thunderstorm. Of course it's great fun hanging on to a metal kite three or four hundred feet up in the middle of a thunderstorm". The place he landed in that scene was covered with thistles, and he spent the next day lying in bed having thorns plucked out of his feet. During the Acid Queen

ROGER DALTREY

sequence he was covered with stick insects, but they had to abandon the idea: "Didn't work did it? They just shit all over me and left. Same with the butterflies—I got covered with butterfly shit, and it don't half pen-and-ink. All for nothing. You wouldn't think little things like that could make a mess like that would you?"

Then again he nearly got burned alive during the scrapyard filming: "Apparently it doesn't look like it, but I did. I lost a load of hair and got burned all up my arm". And he nearly drowned when he had to dive to the bottom of a sixteen-foot pool for the 'I'm Free' sequence so they could shoot from the observation windows. "The only way I could get down was to breathe out so there was no air in my lungs: I got down there all right . . . but it was a bit near really. I was stood on the bottom thinking 'how the fuck am I going to get up again?' and it seemed to take forever. When I finally broke the water half the stage crew were stripped off ready to go in for me".

He likes working for Ken Russell does he? "He gives, so much back that it's a pleasure to do it, it's so rewarding to do it".

Ken Russell was the director Roger wanted to make the film of 'Tommy' from the moment the idea of making it into a film came up. "I'd seen a lot of his TV stuff and I wanted 'Tommy' to be like that". It's a long time since the idea was first thought of, but Daltrey reckons it has been worth the wait. "As it worked out, I don't think Ken would have been right for it years ago, but I think he is now . . . what's so good about it is that it's very real, and yet surreal. 'Tommy' needs to be a classic, and I think it'll become a classic: I think we've all succeeded in doing at least what I wanted to do with it. We didn't need to make a film of it unless it was going to be a classic, because the music sells forever anyway and as soon as you put visuals to it you've made a satement. It's a very dangerous thing to do as far as we were concerned as The Who. But I think he'll get his classic out of it. I think it's worked out just right—a breath of fresh air for us and for him".

Daltrey compares working with Russell on the film with working with Kit Lambert on the original album: "He really gives you confidence and pushes out energy, but it's not just that: it's giving you the feeling that you're part of something that's right, that's good and that's going to be big, which is what everybody needs. Making the film actually became a bit like making an album —we had the basic story and just built on it as we went along. I enjoyed almost every minute". Among the most successful sequences he feels are the Pinball Wizard with Elton John—"because the crowd were so good"—and the Preacher/Marilyn Monroe thing with Eric Clapton—"because of its weirdness". The Acid Queen he regards as brilliant: "It puts something into 'Tommy' in a strange way. One of the things we realised while we were making the film was that Tommy never really makes a statement or does a great deal, but somehow that Acid Queen sequence makes him seem less hollow".

On the subject of potentially 'controversial' sections of the film, he says: "I don't think the violence is vicious. Even the Cousin Kevin sequence is more inferred than actual —and it's much more effective than seeing someone beat the fuck out of someone else. Ken made the symbolism very surreal in places—I think he stretches a point here and there in the original story to make his point, but that's what he's good at". And the use of cripples? "Knowing the reaction there was in some areas of the Press to our original story of a deaf, dumb and blind boy, I'm sure that will be misunderstood by some people. But what should the man have done? Dressed people up to look like cripples? Pretended they don't exist? For some of them it was one of the most interesting fortnights of their lives when they were working on the film—they were expensive extras and patient people who worked hard and seemed to enjoy it".

If the film is going to resurrect Daltrey as the Tommy persona, it is also going to bring a renewed barrage of those 'what does it mean?' questions. That isn't a prospect he relishes: "That'll drive me up the wall—I still don't know what it means. It happened on the first day of the film and it blew my mind: I'm too close to it, it's like trying to answer what it's like to be married. For the first six months you can give some kind of sensible answer, but after ten years it's almost impossible. It's part of my life. I think the spiritual message is made quite clear by Russell—the beginning and end are important, and the ways Tommy's message is twisted and he's ripped off by everyone in sight come over quite clearly. In some ways it's just like the rock business—the group, which is the main source of earnings and goodwill, is usually accused of ripping off the public at some stage of their success, and usually they're the last people to rip anyone off. It's the people on the way to and from the group who're responsible for most of that".

Daltrey was much involved in the planning of the final scene where Tommy's followers finally get the message that they're being conned rotten by the organisation, and they rebel. "It's a frustration thing I've always had inside me about politics, revolutionaries and all that. People dream about revolution and all that crap, but really what they are is like the end of 'Tommy'—dead people, destruction and nothing. That's what revolutions really are. They ripped everybody off, the people rebelled, that's the end result".

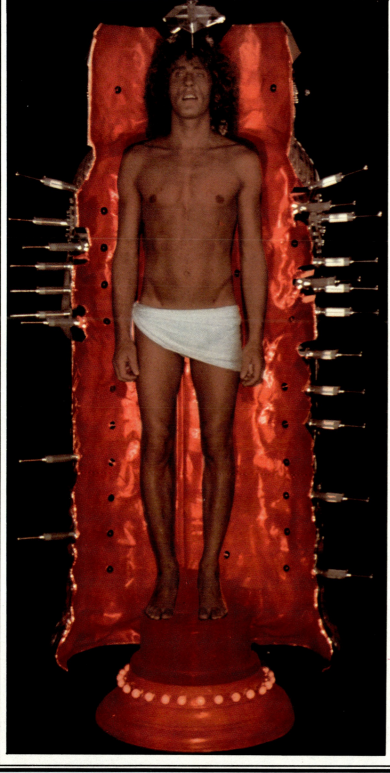

Sally Simpson

Outside the house Mr. Simpson announced
That Sally couldn't go to the meeting
He went on cleaning his black Rolls Royce and
She ran inside weeping

She got to her room and tears splashed
The picture of the new Messiah
She picked up a book of her father's life
And threw it on the fire

She knew from the start
Deep down in her heart
That she and Tommy were worlds apart
But her mother said, never mind, your part
Is to be what you'll be

The theme of the sermon was "Come Unto Me"
Love will find a way
So Sally decided to ignore her dad
And sneak out anyway

She spent all afternoon getting ready
And decided she'd try to touch him
Maybe he'd see that she was free
And talk to her this Sunday

She knew from the start
Deep down in her heart
She and Tommy were worlds apart
But her mother said, never mind, your part
Is to be what you'll be

She arrived at six
and the place was swinging
to gospel music by nine
Group after group appeared on the stage
and Sally just sat there sighing
She bit her nails looking pretty as a picture
Right in the very front row
One of the faithful came on the stage
and shouted "Here we go!"

The crowd went crazy
As Tommy hit the stage!
Little Sally got lost as the police bossed
the crowd back in a rage!

*Your happy welcome is like a favour
I must now return
The darkness of my childhood passed
And flames of love now burn
The pinball games I play so well
Reflects a way of life
This meeting is just another game
Let's play to win tonight*

She knew from the start
Deep down in her heart
She and Tommy were worlds apart
But her mother said, never mind, your part
Is to be what you'll be
Her cheek hit a chair and blood trickled down
Mingling with her tears

*Try to walk the path I walked
– never mind the pain and fear
each one of you has freedom
in your heart – without my grace,
Let me see you raise your hands
See joy upon your face*

The crowd went crazy
As Tommy left the stage!
Little Sally was lost for the price of a touch
And a gash across her face!
Ooooooooooh!
Her pretty face! Ooooooooooh!

Sixteen stitches put her right and her dad said,
Don't say I didn't warn yer!
Sally got married to a rock musician
Who came from California

Tommy always talks about the day
The disciples all went wild
Sally still carries a scar on her cheek
To remind her of his smile

She knew from the start
Deep down in her heart
She and Tommy were worlds apart
But her mother said, never mind, your part
Is to be what you'll be.

ANN-MARGRET

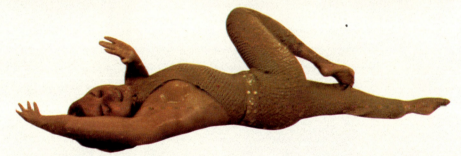

"She actually has a very tough, physical quality about her, and the kind of qualities that made Glenda Jackson a star".—Ken Russell.

"She really should make a rock and roll album. I think she's excellent and she has really suffered from the image which some of her early films have given her. She has this cabaret-showbusiness image, and she's really not like that at all".—Roger Daltrey.

"She's a very, very, very sweet person but it's not a sex thing with her—she's like an angel. Both Russell and I fell madly in love with her and I don't think any of us proposed that she go to the bed".—Oliver Reed.

"That lovely girl with huge boobs..."—Keith Moon.

Ann-Margaret sees Nora Walker, Tommy's Mother, as: "a woman who goes through many changes over the years, from a fresh innocent young girl into a hard, greedy and guilty woman, but who finally finds her own salvation. I think (the film) is about two words—finding God.

"It's a marvellous part, one of the best I've ever had, and working with Ken Russell is incredible—he's brilliant and demanding and at the same time stimulating and understanding".

Perhaps it's not the part you'd immediately associate with Ann-Margret. She started in films as Bette Davis' daughter in 'A Pocketful Of Miracles' in 1961, starred in the Rodgers and Hammerstein 'State Fair' the next year, and went on to play lovely girls with huge boobs opposite people like Dick Van Dyke ('Bye Bye Birdie'), Elvis Presley ('Viva Las Vegas'), Steve McQueen ('The Cincinatti Kid'), Dean Martin ('Murderers' Row'), Bing Crosby ('Stagecoach') and Anthony Quinn ('RPM'). Along with her cabaret shows and TV programmes, perhaps 'personality' would have been a more apt description than 'actress'.

But then she made 'Carnal Knowledge' with Mike Nichols directing and Jack Nicholson as co-star. She was nominated for an Academy award, and gained respect for her abilities as an actress. Ken Russell offered her the part as Nora Walker in October before shooting began, and he has asked her to work with him again.

"I was genuinely excited about it", she says, "because it was so different from the roles I'm normally offered, and I've always admired Ken Russell's work.

"The idea of having to sustain a character throughout an entire film without dialogue was a real challenge. I only knew about The Who from my step-children, but I had heard 'Tommy' and the more I got into the concept, the more fascinated I became.

"The further I got into the character of the Mother the more interesting and intense it became. She really starts out as quite an uncomplicated and attractive personality but gradually the guilt builds up, and the awareness of what she has done to her little boy and what he becomes affects her, and she becomes harder and more callous.

"I realised that every day was going to bring something new to the role when I met Ken, because he likes you to come to the scene with an idea and then build on that at the time. That way you get spontaneity and freshness in the approach. He taught me a lot about myself and my craft".

Was she worried about working with a director of Russell's volatile reputation?

"He is a very complex man, and he has his moments when he is extremely demanding, but he always gives his best and I think he expects the same of his cast. It takes time to get to know him and what he wants but once you have established that communication is there forever—you know almost without asking. I'm sure that's the reason he likes to work with the same people in so many of his films. If he has got to know the actors and they know him, it saves all the time and trouble of having to explain himself and his requirements.

"I think you can place what interpretation you like upon Townshend's lyrics, but this is obviously very much Russell's interpretation. I think it retains the spirituality and I think it is a very inspirational film. It ends on such a high pitch, happy and with hope, that it left me feeling elated despite some of the heavy intensity of earlier scenes.

"There's certainly one sequence I'll never forget, which involved a scene where I am sitting in this totally white room drinking champagne and getting very smashed. I'm watching 'Tommy' on TV now that he is the Pinball Champion and making a lot of money. I start out lying on this scrumptious white satin bed with white walls and white carpet, wearing a silver catsuit dripping with diamonds.

"As I become steadily drunker and more maudlin watching my son on TV—the commercials become mixed up with the programme and gradually I begin to realise that all his fame and fortune is worth nothing if he cannot see, hear or speak".

After she'd finished filming, the crew gave her a chef's hat and apron, emblazoned with the word 'Slugger'. Ann-Margret can't cook, and she earned her self-imposed nickname with a reputation for having accidents while she's working.

"It's a well known fact", says Oliver Reed, "that if you get Russell and Reed together in a film, usually you can sell it anywhere". So he isn't just what you might call modest. Equally he isn't a man to nurse delusions about himself.

He has compared his face to a dustbin, and described his general image as "the looks of a Bedford truck with the promise of a V8 engine".

A standing joke among film people is that Ken Russell loves to work with Reed because he knows exactly what he can get: "Okay Ollie, moody number eight". It's a somewhat harsh over-simplification when you consider the variety of rôles Reed has played, with and without Russell, but doubtless Reed would appreciate the implication of professionalism in his craft.

"I'm exactly the same as I was—the burly ex-public schoolboy with the moody face. What I've done is I've slowed up a bit, my deliveries aren't intense as they used to be: I've always said that if in doubt, do absolutely nothing".

One of his first breaks was in children's television and his first starring role was in Hammer's 'The Curse Of The Werewolf' from which he went on to star in six other Hammer films, which he regards as his apprenticeship. His "intellectual breakthrough" was as Debussy in Ken Russell's TV film about the composer, and his 'the man women of all ages would like to give them the once over' reputation was firmly established with his performance in Russell's 'Women In Love': not only did Glenda Jackson get the Ollie treatment, but he wrestled naked, by firelight, with Alan Bates.

"Since then", says Reed, "I've hardly been offered a script in which I haven't been asked to take my clothes off, but I won't do it again". He does, however, enjoy being able to say that a million women saw him naked. While making 'Tommy' he was voted Britain's sexiest actor by readers of *Photo-play* magazine, and he is fond of saying that he engenders a violent reaction in women. They either love or hate him, and most love him he says. "You don't have to have classical good looks to be a movie star anymore. I was lucky enough to become established in the mid-sixties when the show-business climate was changing, and had been ever since John Osborne wrote 'Look Back In Anger': the rough working class, regional-accented hero—or anti-hero—was in the ascendent. You didn't have to look like John Mills or Michael Redgrave or Dirk Bogarde to get on".

Oliver Reed is hardly a rough, working class, regional-accented anti-hero. His mode of private life is that of a right-wing English country gentleman, his house is a converted monastery in Surrey with something like 50 acres of land giving him a 20-mile, uninterrupted view of the countryside and a seven-acre lake. He works hard, doing about three films a year, is fiercely proud of his earning power, is divorced, and doesn't like women to be clever. "I hope I'm clever enough for both of us". He breeds horses, would like to be the owner of the best showjumper, the best heavyweight hunter and the Derby winner all in the same year. He says he doesn't have aspirations to direct films, not yet anyway, but he does have plans to be a producer. His criteria for accepting a film part are: "if it's a good worthwhile part, the script and general set-up smell right, and—very important this—the money's good. Then I'll go ahead".

He says he's a romantic, and of his house he says: "it's an escape for me, I love the space and opulence. If I have a row with my girlfriend, neither of us need walk out—we can go off into separate wings and not come across one another for days, even weeks".

And when he surveys his minor armoury of guns, both antique and modern, saying "I think I could hold my own here, I'm the last of the warlords" you feel that it might not be entirely in jest. Oliver Reed wouldn't look kindly on an uprising of peasants and welfare-state spongers. Pete Townshend found that one of the easiest ways to get a rise out of him on the set was to yell 'Vote Labour': Ollie spent much of the time in his caravan listening to Radio Four, occasionally emerging to engage the carpenters in conversation about the burden of his taxes.

He has a fine sense of the bawdy, as is illustrated by his 'erotic bet' with a barmaid at his local pub; if he could lose two stone in weight in a month, she was prepared to allow him unrestricted access to her ample breasts for ten minutes. The burly ex-public schoolboy with a moody face was observed sucking a baby's dummy—"in training" for his prize, he said, and presumably also to stop the food getting through.

But as an actor in his late thirties, Oliver Reed is now prepared to relinquish romance, in the sense of having beautiful women melt into his warm embrace as he Exudes Earthy Sensuality From His Burly Frame. Frank may be the Lover in 'Tommy', but Reed plays him—to a certain extent—for laughs. "I'm getting older now. I think it worries everybody terribly when they're 27 that maybe they're not as sexy as they should be, but I think when you reach 37 you're not really that concerned. Nobody wants to see a 40 year old fat man kissing an 18 year old girl, but everyone loves to see a 40-year-old fat man making them cry, frightening them or amusing them. My parts are beginning to change as I get older—I've done all my kissing and I've sucked Glenda Jackson's knockers enough to last me a lifetime, God bless her. No, it doesn't worry me—had I tried to make Frank into a romantic I would have failed, because he shouldn't be a romantic".

The part of Frank was fairly nebulous at the start, and in fact was much smaller than it ended up. Russell, however, felt that Reed's experience should be used more fully, and Frank took over a lot of business from Uncle Ernie (Keith Moon). It was Townshend's intial reaction to his singing that gave Reed the clue to his portrayal of Frank:

"I sang a few notes and Townshend fell about laughing in the studio—you see you can't take Frank seriously in the film so I made him a sort of caricature, but not so ridiculous that he bceomes unbelievable. He can't be a bully, and I didn't want him to be a bully, I wanted people to maybe identify with him, have a laugh with him, and feel a little sorry for him".

The sequence with the specialist for instance, is played with Frank putting on airs and graces in an almost pathetic way, and

OLIVER REED

Reed admits to nicking a bit for it from the Butler in one of his earlier films, 'Blue Blood'. He had Frank trying to match the Specialist's suave Harley Street manner, and only looking uncomfortable. And he played on the fact that he is not a singer.

"Who's that flourishing American actor? Jack Nicholson. He seemed to think it was my normal voice, and his only comment was 'I don't think I'm a very good singer (Townshend says he came out as smooth as Perry Como) but I'm certainly a better singer than Oliver Reed'. Which somewhat missed the point".

Reed enjoys the freedom of his part: "It was great fun because I could play with the part and go way over the top . . . there's no way you can go over the top in 'Tommy' with the Who's music and Ken Russell's directing. I mean if I was to take my cock out as I did in 'Women In Love' and stick it up a turkey's bum, it's not over the top. Vanessa Redgrave shoved a crucifix up her's in "The Devils". In a sense it's cocking a snook at all the sort of things I wanted to do . . ."

The way Reed was able to shape his part in the film is in some way typical of the way Russell likes actors to work with him. One of the standard comments about Russell from his actors is that he encourages them to come to him with ideas. A frequent comment from other people is that he's 'volatile'.

"He is", says Reed "but when he gets volatile I usually shout back at him and take him quietly aside and tell him he's being unreasonable. Usually he then comes back and says in front of people "I'm sorry". Ken had a nervous breakdown. He's one of these incredibly talented people who lives off nervous energy and he needs to be understood—that is he needs people around him who understand his moods. Ken has an amazing photographic eye, and he used to be a dancer. There are very few times when I need direction from him now, so he can get on with other things and not have to worry about me. For him that's one problem out of the way.

"A lot of directors like to work closely with actors and actresses, but Ken likes working with the camera, concentrating on movement, the way you move, the way the light falls.

In a lot of ways then, the actors took care of themselves: "The Who knew their lines, Roger Daltrey knows how to work, and you only have to capture one third of Moon's enthusiasm and push him in the right direction. I've worked with Ken enough to know what he wants, and Ann-Margret is a real pro—we all fell madly in love with her".

Reed might reasonably be expected to be intolerant of 'amateurs' on the set—it was Roger Daltrey's first film after all. But Daltrey proved himself enough for Russell to cast him as Liszt in his next picture, and he proved himself in Reed's eyes as well. "You have to learn certain discipline as an actor and Roger was very professional and enthusiastic. He also seems able to contain that enthusiasm in front of the camera, which is terribly important.

"And it's no use coming on, as one person did, and just because you happen to be called on set at eight in the morning and you aren't required until 7.15pm you get stoned out of your mind. Moon had practically to stick a broom up that man's behind to keep him upright. You have to be ready when required. The only actors who could get away with that kind of behaviour were big Hollywood stars, because the people came to see them and not the film.

"I think Roger has a seriously quality about him which will enable him to make the transition to films—there hasn't really been a singer who's done it since Frank Sinatra. Paul Jones tried from Manfred Mann, but he was too nice, like jelly and ice cream is nice. You have to have a bit of nasty to make it. And I remember making 'Beat Girl' with Adam Faith—he's a constant surprise to me, because every time they say he's got away and learned something new he comes back and to me he's Adam Faith, he's just the same as he ever was. Either you've got to accept that his style of acting is in vogue or it is not: there's no way that everybody can keep pretending that they've discovered Adam Faith".

Off the set, Reed formed a friendship with Keith Moon which was compared to a meeting between King Kong and Godzilla. "Daltrey said that over the period of the film, although Moon did some crazy things, he was very quiet and contented. I could absorb a lot of his lunacy, the same as I can with Ken.

"At first they were going to separate us during shooting, by putting me in one hotel and Moon in another, but then they decided the best thing would be to put us both in the same hotel but away from the posh people. We found ourselves billetted with the plasterers and chippies, which was marvellous because they were much more our kind of people. Moon has enormous energy and great enthusiasm". (Townshend gets angry that people will not accept Moon as superhuman).

"He lives life at an incredibly fast rate and lives it to the full. I remember he found a novel way of summoning the night porter at one hotel where they boasted 24 hour room service, and he was unable to get a bottle of brandy at 3am as there was no reply from the desk. He simply lobbed the colour TV out of his 14th-floor window, and the fellow was upstairs in seconds.

"I think I finally made my mark on Moon though. I taught him to say 'certainly' and 'Madam would you mind?' in the most cultured tones, and I gave him a tortoise called Shell that he's quite devoted to".

The affinity with Moon in one way is mirrored with Reed's affinity with Ken Russell in another; and where Moon's aggression and energy often find expression on stage with the Who, Russell's often comes out in his films. "I think everybody is what life or their environment allows them to be. Russell's life has probably been traumatic and I think the figures and characters he meets in his bouts of depression and in his nightmare frighten him so much that he puts them into movies".

As a kind of exorcism perhaps. Reed feels he might represent one of those figures to Russell in a way: "I think I'm one he thinks he could meet and knows he could drink with afterwards, and that probably makes him a little bit happier when next he dreams".

WELCOME

Come to my house
Be one of the comfortable people
Come to this house
We're drinking all night
Never sleeping

Milkman come in
And you baker
Little old lady welcome
And you Shoemaker
Come to this house
Into this house

Come to this house
Be one of us
Make this your house
Be one of us

You can help
To collect some more in
Young and old people
Let's get them all in
Come to this house
Into this house

Ask along that man with a big red carnation
Bring every single person from Victoria Station
Go into the hospital and bring the nurses and patients
Everyone go home
and fetch their relations

Come into this house
Be one of the comfortable people
Lovely bright home
We're drinking all night
Never sleeping

Hold on Tommy
There's more at the door
They'll come through the floor
There's more at the door
There's more at the door
There's more at the door
There's more at the door
There's more at the door
There's more . . .

We need more room
Build an extension
A colourful palace
Spare no expense now

Come to me now
Come to me now
Welcome! Welcome!
Welcome!

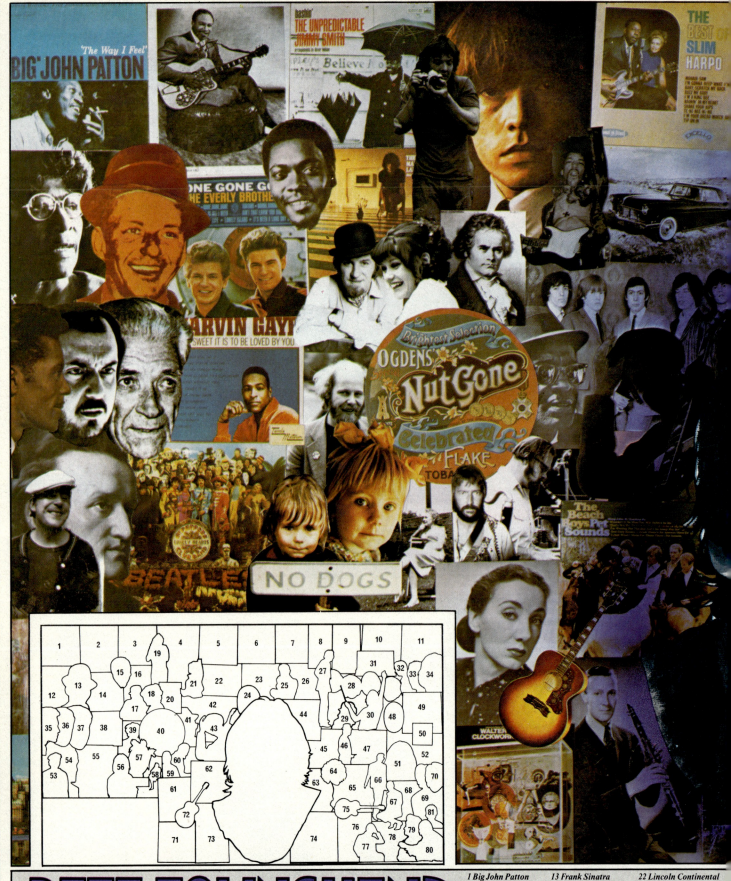

PETE TOWNSHEND

(Above) A portrait of Pete Townshend surrounded by the records, musicians, composers, businessmen, family, friends, things and others that have most influenced him. Richard Barnes, who has known Pete Townshend on and off for fifteen years, compiled the list (which Pete later amended and added to). On the next page he interviews Pete on influences that led to the writing of Tommy.

1 Big John Patton
2 Jimmy Reed
3 Jimmy Smith
4 Brian Jones
5 Slim Harpo
6 Jimmy Giuffre
7 Bo Diddley
8 Ray Charles
9 Mose Allison
10 Wes Montgomery
11 Terry Riley
12 Ella Fitzgerald
13 Frank Sinatra
14 Everly Brothers
15 Booker T & The MG's
16 Syd Barrett
17 Acker Bilk
18 Karen Townshend (Pete's wife)
19 Tom Wright (turned Pete onto dope and blues music)
20 Beethoven
21 Jimi Hendrix
22 Lincoln Continental cars
23 John Lee Hooker
24 Bach
25 Debussy
26 Bob Druce (manager of The Detours)
27 Robert Stigwood
28 The Beatles
29 Ken Russell
30 Keith Moon
31 EMS synthesiser

32 Chris Stamp and...
33 Kit Lambert
34 Andrew Oldham
35 Chuck Berry
36 Stanley Kubrick
37 George Adamski (UFO traveller)
38 Marvin Gaye
39 Bobby Pridden (Who sound man)
40 Ogdens' Nutgone LP (& The Small Faces)

41 Lightnin' Hopkins
42 Rolling Stones
43 Bob Dylan
44 Kenny Burrell
45 Chet Atkins
46 Bill Graham
47 Snooks Eaglin
48 Purcell
49 The Incredible String Band
50 Nik Cohn (pop writer)
51 John Entwistle

52 The River Thames
53 Pete Meadon (manager of The High Numbers)
54 Wagner
55 Sgt. Pepper
56 Aminta Townshend (youngest daughter)
57 Emma Townshend (eldest daughter)
58 Denny (Pete's grandmother)

59 Eric Clapton
60 Thunderclap Newman
61 Betty Townshend (Pete's mother)
62 Pet Sounds LP and The Beach Boys
63 Guy Stevens (turned Pete onto early Sue records and U.S. R&B
64 Roger Daltrey
65 Mr. Fantasy LP and Traffic

66 Hank Marvin and...
67 Bruce Welch
68 Green Onions LP
69 Speedy Keen (friend and musician)
70 Mike McInnerney (turned Pete onto Meher Baba)
71 Walter Carlos
72 Gibson J200 guitar
73 Cliff Townshend (Pete's dad)

74 Aftermath LP
75 Gretch 'Chet Atkins' guitar
76 Rupert Bear
77 Tchaikovsky
78 The Kinks
79 Delia deLeon (Life-long devotee of Meher Baba)
80 Elgar
81 Richard Barnes (friend)

Also but not shown:—
Ronnie Lane
Rickenbacker guitars
Irish Jack (friend)
Simon & Paul Townshend (Pete's brothers)
Ray Tolliday
Don Stevens (writer on Meher Baba)
Colin Jones (Observer photographer)
Lowrie organs

Gustav Metzke (auto-destructive artist)
Bosendorfer pianos
Murshida Ivy Duce (head of American Sufi group)
Pepe Rush (electronics specialist)
Dr. Alan Cohen (one-time LSD advocate, and now a Baba follower)
Towser (Pete's dog)
And those we've missed

In the late sixties Pete Townsend became increasingly interested and intrigued by the teachings of Meher Baba. He was even more impressed by Meher Baba, the man, and although he never met Meher Baba personally Pete says he "fell in love with him".

Richard Barnes has been a close friend of Townshend since they met and shared a flat together at art school in 1961. He says "I noticed an incredible change in Townshend and his wife Karen about the time they were discovering Meher Baba. I was quite impressed." Here Richard Barnes talks to Pete Townshend about 'Tommy', Meher Baba, The Who and Pete Townshend.

When you started writing 'Tommy' were you into Meher Baba? Was it as a result of Baba?

I can't remember exact details but I know that what had happened was that I had come out of that sort of incredible LSD experience that I had in Monterey, and that in a way made me think that I'd been knocking myself about a bit with drugs, and I started to feel this strange sort of responsibility for myself in a spiritual way, and I thought I must really pull myself and my life together. At that time I was knocking about with Arthur Brown a lot, and we were talking about an opera. I wrote a thing 'Rael' which Kit Lambert condensed down to sort of a five minute thing; it was originally a grand, lengthy operatic thing. So I think I was thinking in terms of not rock opera, but in terms of proper opera. I was studying orchestrations and stuff like that, and I'd bought a piano, and then I did a lot of orchestrations and I bought lots of books about it and I used to speak a lot to Karen's Dad about orchestrations and stuff like that.

A reason I was interested in Arthur Brown

DON'T WORRY — BE HAPPY.
—Meher Baba

(Above and top) Meher Baba the silent master who became the spiritual focus for Pete Townshend and the inspiration for much of the writing of Tommy. When showed an early picture of 'The Who' on the cover of THE OBSERVER colour magazine, Baba apparently pressed his thumb on Townshend's nose. Although Meher Baba was always joking and playing tricks, this action was thought by some to have some mystical significance. Certainly Townshend has been 'under his thumb' ever since, although he never met Baba.

was because I thought he had an amazing sort of rock/operatic voice and he was going to be the star of it, as it were. Then the time came that the Who needed an album and Kit Lambert's method of getting new material—because I never wrote anything specifically for the Who ever in my life, it always happens to be what I'm into at the particular time—is just to steam in and pick up what we had, and he sort of engineered it into this rock opera thing. I was, simultaneously to all this, finding out a lot about Baba. It's hard to say, it all happened at the same time. For example I had written a lot of the songs before we moved to Richmond and I know that when we moved to Richmond it was about the time that this fascination with Baba became really concrete. I know that it all happened in the space of two months, one minute I was freaked out on acid the next minute I was into Baba. But the fascination with opera and even with 'Tommy' as a concept (it was originally called 'Amazing Journey') was all happening at the same time.

Originally the 'Amazing Journey' was the story of a sort of seeker, and you saw his life in reality and in a dream, that sort of thing. You've got a double-barrelled plot—one minute you'd see him from one angle objectively, and the other minute you'd see him from the other angle subjectively, so one song followed another song, followed another song, followed another song. Originally for example the section in 'Tommy' where you've got 'Cousin Kevin', 'Fiddle About', 'Acid Queen', and stuff like that, each one was going to be followed by sort of an impressionistic dream-sequence-type piece of music like the 'Underture'. In the end me just had the one. See I was reading things like Herman Hesse, and stuff like that, before I really got into Baba. I had heard about Baba but I wasn't really into all his stuff. I'd just read a few books.

To me 'Tommy' is very much a Meher Baba story, especially things like Tommy being deaf dumb and blind. Maybe I was reading more into it than was intended, but isn't his blindness and deafness meant to be some kind of an analogy with for instance, the fact that we don't exactly experience reality. We are conditioned by habit patterns and things and can only experience what they allow us to experience. And we are, say, blind and deaf to reality, Tommy is a literal example of somebody in that position,

When I first started writing 'Tommy' he was not deaf, dumb and blind. The first song that I wrote—'Amazing Journey', that was the absolute first song of 'Tommy'—that was like the pivot point and as a song it more or less tells you everything that you want to know about the story of 'Tommy'. You know "deaf, dumb and blind boy, he's in a strange vibration land" etc, etc. What the lyrics really mean is that though he can only feel things, from these feelings they become like music to him, and the music that he sort of feels and the vibrations become important to him, and it becomes like his guide and his leader and his master. I was actually going to try to cope with this on quite a grand scale, I was going to try to create pieces of music which represented his feelings at any given point, but him being deaf, dumb and blind initially was just a sort of thing I grabbed out of the air.

Why?

I don't know really, I think either it might have been for the reason that you said, that I wanted to make him kind of remote, but on the other hand it might just have come out of the sky. I just don't know, because a lot of ideas that I had, songs like 'Substitute' for example (which I now look back on and I reckon is one of the best lyrics that I've ever written) I just wrote out the top of my head and I don't really know what motivated it.

I thought Tommy being deaf, dumb and blind was there for some definite reasons. Like you were saying, there are these two situations; there's Tommy's experiences on the one hand, and what other people outside are seeing, looking at this remote deaf, dumb and blind kid, on the other. A subjective and objective thing. I never sat down and thought about the story line of 'Tommy' but I always got the impression that he was meant to be like Mr. Average, walking around in his own little dream, and really he's deaf, dumb and blind to reality. He can only experience what he can experience.

As the theme developed, that's exactly what I did, and that's exactly what I meant to happen. What eventually then emerged was that I ended up with the parallel, it's almost like a device. The device was that when he came out of his autism and became normal, that was then such a miracle to him that that in itself pushed him beyond normality and into a sort of Saintlihood, and because his experience in that state was quite unique . . . I mean I just see that as a little device, it's not really all that important. I think there were three or four devices that I used in the thing like that; there's the deaf, dumb and blind thing paralleled to the fact that we're only an illusion. It was the mirror, the fact that he could only see himself (this being a thing about the ego), but also the fact that he sees himself and the image that he sees in the mirror he takes to be someone else, he doesn't say 'that's me'. But when his Mother finally smashes the mirror, and he sees himself disappearing, he realises that that person he sees as God is himself, and so the actual complete God-realisation from that is effected. The other devices are like the pain and the pleasure and things like that.

One other device which I'd actually forgotten about is the whole thing about Pinball; that now to me seems just as daft as it does to everybody else, but originally I had some real reason for having Pinball, it did come from Nick Cohn originally and it was a bit of a gag, but I had some reason why I used it as a device. It was something to do with it being a game but also it was to do with his music thing, the fact that everything he felt sort of came through as very pure, simple vibrations which he would hear as music. I got the idea that something like the Pinball game, like what you would feel when you played Pinball, would make a good sort of musical piece and it went on and off from there, it got deeper and deeper. Then I started to get into the whole thing about life is a game, and the essence of the game, and the importance of little games like that, as I read that Baba was interested in games.

I thought you picked on Pinball because it was so trivial. I thought you didn't want to get involved with anything philosophical or anything like that.

That again is true because as I went along I retrospectively weighed everything that I'd done because I had to do that to incorporate a lot of material. I had songs like 'Sally Simpson' for example, and 'We're Not Going To Take It'—they were already written as individual songs and I incorporated them into 'Tommy'. 'Welcome' was a song that was written before 'Tommy', 'I'm Free' was written before 'Tommy', 'Sensation' was written before 'Tommy'. All these were written just as songs and it was only when I started to look around and I realised . . . what I'm saying is, it's very difficult for me to say "Oh yes I planned it all", because in a way a fantastic magic was going on. But then that always happens with me, and I think it's not quite so mystic as it appears on the surafce. I think at the back of your head something is going on that you're not aware of and it makes you write in a certain way. If you mass everything together that you've written over a year you'll find it will all have a certain quality to it, and maybe even a theme running through.

You did say that you were slightly interested in mysticism and people that are interested will get out of it what they can. I mean if Bob Dylan sang, 'I'm A Blue Toothbrush, You're Pink Toothbrush' a lot of people would get a lot of deep meaning from that.

Well I get a fantastic amount of deep feeling from 'Mighty Quinn', a fantastic amount. I find it to be the most spiritual evocative song. It suggests to me that thing about the spiritual hierarchy and I hear the music and I think of this great big sort of Baba as an Eskimo sitting on top of the world.

Obviously you don't sit down and coldly calculate that 'Tommy' is going to be a spiritual message or anything like that, but what I was saying was that people are going to read into it what they want, and at that time when everybody was getting into that sort of thing it was a good focus for them.

Well, I'll tell you something really funny: at the time that we were writing 'Tommy' the music business was very much like it is at the moment—it was very super-cynical. For example, at that time the Moody Blues and people were doing ambitious works, from their point of view anyway, and they were instantly getting labelled as pretentious and at the same time garbage was being pushed out into the charts. The Beatles and The Stones and people like that, the Small Faces even—anybody that was any good was more or less becoming insignificant again. They weren't new anymore, they weren't fresh, and a lot of the new stuff that was coming out was really trash, there was a lot of psychedelic bullshit going about. All the main people, like I suppose the Who and the Stones and the Beatles, were all involved in acid and were very sort of insipid and sort of weak fundamentally, as far as the public were concerned, as a result. What I wanted to do at that particular time was to be sort of musico-diplomatic, I wanted to hit everybody all at once. So I did, cautiously, put across a spiritual message because I did feel that I had learnt a fantastic amount through my life and perhaps even through dope, which had led me to Baba, and I knew that Baba was something very special and I wanted this all to be wound up. But at the same time I wanted 'Tommy' to be rock and roll, I wanted it to be like singles that you could pull out and play. You could pull out 'I'm Free' and 'Sensation' and they'd be good just as songs. I didn't really want the thing to have any musical flow, you know like themes connecting it, I just wanted it to be a series of singles that happened to tell a story. I even wanted it to appeal to kids. John Entwistle and I always used to talk a lot about that . . . like his thing about horror songs, and stuff like that, the whole thing about how kids are really into that sort of thing, Grimm's fairy tales, that John always used to justify his black humour.

We just wanted it to appeal on every level. Like a Sufi tale—one of those tales of the dervishes. It's a good story in itself, it's exciting, it's got a beginning, a middle and an end. It's a good story from the point of view of it being ethnic in quality, a Persian thing, it's beautifully written, yet at the same time deep down below is a thread. If you're a seeker you get something from it, if you're well along the path you get something from it, and even somebody like Baba, who's at the absolute pinnacle of realisation, you can look at something like that and see some beauty in it, see something special in it. That was really what I was trying to aim at with 'Tommy' so that even somebody who wasn't interested at all in spiritual matters would still be able to dig it.

Yes, I think for instance a Marxist could relate to 'Tommy' and see it in terms of a class struggle. Atheists and humanists could see the liberation of man or something. All kinds of people could identify with something in it, not because it's there but because it has a simple enough and strong enough story line. it's also sufficiently vague. I always thought 'Tommy' vague. I never knew what it was going on about. This might have been one of the reasons for its success, and might have saved it from appearing incredibly pretentious.

I think you're absolutely right. I get really irritated today that if in a rock song you actually mention anything specifically that is considered very bad in rock terms. You know, hitting something head-on. You're supposed to skirt round it and flirt round it in a way say that a Stones lyric would, and maybe mention it in a sort of double-meaning, double-edged vague way. I've always been very frustrated with this aspect of rock, I don't get anything from that type of song. I think that the great sort of strata of rock critique if you like, has not changed in the years since I wrote 'Tommy'. They're still the same, I think they prefer things to be fairly open ended so that they can lay their own thing into it. What it's doing, and I think this is something I've more recently discovered, is it's bringing music which had merits and a message nearer to the universality of an instrumental piece. Like if you sit down and listen to a piece of Debussy, one person can see the Arctic and another can see the Russian Revolution, you can see anything you like because there's nothing suggested by it other than in a musical way. When you've got words, "I walked into the room and I picked up my spade, and I work for the Revolution" type of thing . . . I mean that is enough to kill anything stone-dead.

You know you were saying you wrote 'I'm Free' before you wrote 'Tommy', but the words to it to me are pure Baba or pure mysticism. It could be Zen, it could be anything . . . "Freedom tastes of Reality" . . . "If I told you what it takes to reach the highest high you'd laugh and say nothing's that simple, but you've been told many times before that Messiahs take you to the door, but no one has the guts to leave the temple". That says a hell of a lot and it doesn't waste any words, and it really isn't vague is it?

I think 'I'm Free' was obviously put together after I'd understood quite a lot about Baba. I think what I was getting at was that I had the chords to it before and I had the 'I'm Free' thing, but I probably originally wrote it as a punk song. 'Sensation' I wrote about a chick I met in Australia, and it was called 'She's A Sensation'. 'Sally Simpson' was about a rock star and it was based on Jim Morrison. I met him in New York and he just absolutely amazed me—some bird went up to talk to him or something, one and of his bodyguards just punched her in the midriff and she doubled up and he just carried on talking, he didn't see her. Then the same afternoon at this club he actually tried to pull this chick, and the way she was . . . I wrote that thing and then realised that in a way he was exactly like what Tommy was, and I just re-wrote it. "We're Not Going To Take It" was a song I'd had knocking about on the cards for ages about fascism.

When the first Who version of 'Tommy' came out, I thought 'We're Not Going To Take It' was about the fact that people wouldn't follow 'Tommy' because they didn't have the patience. They wanted the rewards without the hard work, they wanted spiritual enlightment and they didn't want to do what Tommy said they had to do, meditate, or whatever it was, and they rejected him. Now in the film, Ken Russell's version has got that they're being conned by Uncle Ernie and Frank and that 'Tommy' doesn't know this, he's not aware of the fact and he's completely innocent. But they don't follow him because they are being ripped off.

That was basically originally the theme. I mean it was a bit of both in a way. It's the way that Ken Russell sees it and a bit of the way you see it.

It wasn't that Tommy was conning them?

No, the whole thing with Tommy was that in the last count in our version he realises that they're being conned and so he hots things up so they'll rebel against him. It's like a sort of crucifixion thing, he sacrifices his own aura to them in order that they can go back to what they were doing before, because he realises that that's the best thing they could be doing. This is this whole thing about "if you follow me" you know; Tommy suddenly goes from this poetic airy-fairy character and suddenly gets tough; he suddenly says "if you want to follow me, you've got to do this, you've got to play pinball, you've got to put earplugs in, if you want to be like me, that is what you have to do, you've got to go through what I did". He knows that to be completely ridiculous, he knows that what they needed to do was to go back to live their lives, but he realised that it had gone too far. All he wanted at first was to welcome people to his house, and allow them to be with him; that was all very nice, but it had got out of hand.

Because they wanted answers?

Yes . . .

But you see, there's sort of a double thing; first of all Tommy gets God-realisation. and when the mirror's smashed he breaks through and gets an amazing spiritual realisation, which other people sense because he becomes a vibration, etc., and they feel this power. Then on the other hand, that is destroyed. It's like a twist at the end of a twist, it's like sticking the knife in and then that's not enough, so you twist the knife as you pull it out. This is what I find is very Meher Baba; Baba sort of gives a clue to something important, and just as you think you understand, you see a little footnote which says "all the above is irrelevant". He always has that twist at the end of everything.

I think that one of the most successful things about the end of 'Tommy' was that Kit

persuaded me to reprise what was originally in the 'Go To The Mirror', the doctor scene, 'See Me, Feel Me' and the 'Listening To You' theme. When it came down to it, what I thought was so incredible about that was that here he was, he was still the same guy, he was still God-realised and all that, but this was now the pain, if you like, and the remoteness and the loneliness and the frustration, plus being God-realised. In other words "I've done it, but now I've got to have the patience and the love to drag the rest of humanity through it" sort of thing. That's really what the whole of the end of it is—that despite the fact he created this big achievement, he's not going to be complete, or not going to be at rest if you like, until everybody is. And that that will never be. Deep down inside of every human being is this feeling that nothing is ever going to be complete, that the circle will never connect, and that that in itself is the secret to infinity, that fact that the circle will never, ever be completed is the knowledge of infinity which we have very dimly at the moment. I think you get it from things like Baba liking that song 'There's A Heartache Following Me', and strange songs like 'Begin the Beguine', and things like that: that the Avatar's role (not that 'Tommy' was ever meant to be an Avatar, as such, or a Messiah), is a remote and lonely one, as well as being an incredibly important and glorious one.

I was amazed when I read Ken Russell's script to find it so close to my original interpretation of 'Tommy',

In the original record when he was staring in the mirror singing "Listening to you. gazing at you" etc, who was he singing to? Was it to himself in the mirror?

No, because the whole thing is at the end, because the people have walked away from him, he suddenly sees himself where he really is, he suddenly realises completely and totally that he's definitely not a Messiah, that he's not a complete person, that he's still got a place to go, and that the place he's got to go, if you like, is total universality. He's very much on the path, but . . .

But doesn't he make a mistake? I got the impression that all along he was fooling himself. He thought that he had reached the stage of God-realization or at least gained an advanced spiritual awareness. Then at the end when he was rejected he finally got the message, And then did he really break through the veil of illusion or whatever and realize there was something bigger than himself.

I suppose that's a possible way of looking at it. I mean I've always imagined from my point of view that the mirror smash was a reverse trauma, that the mother is an important sort of key, a sort of symbol in a way, but the most important thing being the mirror. In my story, he witnesses the thing in the mirror. In my story, I imagine that he didn't actually go to the room, there was just a mirror by the door and he witnesses the murder in the mirror, and this is where the whole importance of the mirror comes in. The only thing that he feels is safe to look at, that won't cause him any problems, is his own reflection, which deep inside he knows is his own reflection, but he's sort of ignorant. So that when it actually comes to the moment of trauma, this whole thing has been building up and the mirror smashes and he sees himself fall into bits, he sees his own image which he's been focused on, that he sort of worships as a sort of leader and a guide and a friend collapse. Then, at that point, he realises a lot of other things about life, in that instant. And the uniqueness of the way that he's been living his life, sort of pushes him. We're all sort of grabbing about, doing our thing and he's in this pure sort of untainted, silent world, and it just flings him out and he comes out a bit ahead. that was really the way I felt it.

Every piece of creative work like 'Tommy' must be to some extent autobiographical, Even a top-ten-songette will reflect something of the writer, Wasn't a lot of 'Tommy' to do with your own experiences?

I don't know. I mean I know the difference between say writing something like 'Tommy' and writing something like 'Substitute'. 'Substitute' is an autobiographical thing, and 'My Generation' is autobiographical, even though I never went through the 'My Generation' type stuff. I was part of it in a way, in a way that I can't really understand, I can't really explain. It wasn't in such a glamorous way, in a street fighting, fucking-round-back-corner way, it was the exact opposite. It was in an un-glamorous, frustrated, school-boy type thing. I think there are two ways I can write, even today;

a lot of the stuff for example on 'Who's Next' was written, not from an autobiographical thing, but from an intellectual point of view. You read something and it impresses you, and I suppose in a way that becomes part of your life. It's the impressions that you've got from something, rather than actually experiencing it.

Yes, but what I was thinking was something like smashing the mirror. Tommy's experience might have been like, for example, your first religious experience, or your first LSD experience, or your first cannabis experience. When you first turn-on with pot, you break through that one point of view you've had all your life, and realise that there are thousands of points of view. You suddenly see that there's a lot more to life than you ever thought, a lot of subtle little things: it's quite an amazing experience— LSD is an even more staggering experience.

I think in a way that the autobiographical bit there would tie-up with the Acid Queen and Cousin Kevin and Uncle Ernie. Uncle Ernie is like the grandmother thing that I had, which I found really quite terrifying, and Cousin Kevin is like just the cruelty that was tied up in school, the taunts, and the Acid Queen thing was quite obviously the thing you get from drugs. Really, to me. despite the fact there was this great mystical thing, the thing that really attracted me about dope, I must admit, and also with acid was its glamour. It might have been a secret glamour, but it did make me feel sort of glamorous and special and sort of different. It was that rather than getting stoned and looking at things and learning about them. That's why I made the Acid Queen such a double-edged thing. On one hand it portrayed the glamour and excitement and the challenge of drugs; and on the other hand I tried to put across the slimy side, which is in you. You know, you can't blame the drug, it's in you, it gets the wrong answers, or makes the wrong reactions.

I also thought that the Acid Queen was a prostitute, a sexual thing too?

Yes, it is because you have to pay for drugs.

Were you an atheist before you got into Meher Baba

Yeah, I think I was. I never talked very much about that sort of thing at college, nor about things like politics. I mean I'd been through that Aldermaston march thing, Ban the Bomb thing, but always playing in some silly trad jazz band in the background. Like everybody and his brother seemed to have had their first fuck on the Aldermarston march, and a lot of people went along for that reason, and I was sort of tied up with that kind of individual. I remember feeling that the sheer acceptance of a God, or of something as nebulous as God, when things like bombs and things like this were going down was somehow irresponsible and evil. I don't know why. That was the kind of consciousness that was going on at the time, that people that believed in God weren't just idiots, but they were irresponsible. I still have arguments now with people who say you're just opting out of your responsibilities, you're not facing up to what's really going on in the world, that there's fucking capitalist oppression, that there are things still to be done. The problem really comes when you start to wonder what Baba means by responsibility—you know, "tend to your worldly duties". Because inside everybody there's not just conscience, there's also motivation, and you get this thing sometimes, that you get so fucking angry with what's going on in the world that you want to do something actual about it. I think this is really one of the things which exploded a bit in 'Tommy' and made me run the risk of appearing pretentious, I thought in the end "well, fuck it, I've got to make some sort of statement about spitituality, because it seems to be the only thing I can do". Because I've been writing so much in the worst way, you know. I think it's a very pertinent point, because, it's perhaps getting a bit too intellectual, but I think that atheistic thinking is often much more humanitarian than mystical thinking, at least on the surface.

Yes, I think that what's going on with someone who is sincerely trying to understand the world and trying to tell the truth, is more important than whether they're an atheist or into mysticism or whatever. Baba says that there are many atheists more advanced on the spiritual path, or whatever, than people who think themselves religious.

I think deep-down that this is everbody's fear, and it's as much my fear as anybody

else, that there is this great temptation to lean towards hypocrisy because there are so many escape clauses that you can give yourself if you want. I think I've learnt a fantastic amount of very hard lessons from the Murshida,* but she also can unwittingly provide me with escape clauses. One sort of thing that I know at the moment which is, I was thinking about this the other day: I really did feel very much under Baba's orders when I was putting 'Tommy' together, I felt in a very fanciful way then, something I wouldn't feel now, that really I was under his thumb. Probably it's more the case now; I know much more about him, I maybe think of him less often, but I'm much more involved in a life which is sort of practical day-by-day wearing things down rather than a kind of flippant love-affair thing. That was really what motivated a lot of what makes 'Tommy' I suppose the most ambitious thing that I've ever got into,

*The Murshida is the name given to the spiritual leader of the sufi movement. Townshend met Murshida Ivy Duce, the 80 year old spiritual teacher and head of 'Sufism Reoriented', a number of times when he visited San Fransisco.

and I don't suppose that I'll ever do anything as ambitious as it again. Take "Quadrophenia": I mean, that was fucking hard enough to get together, and that was just a story of a day in the life of a punk, let alone getting something together which is the day in the life of a punk **and** the history of society **and** childhood **and** this and that **and** mysticism . . .

It must have taken a vast amount of energy and hard graft. How the hell did you do it?

It just sort of came together. I think a lot of it just has to come back to Baba, it just has to, because it's an open and shut case. What was different about that particular time was that it was that period when Baba takes you by the scruff of the neck and shows you what your potential is, you know what I mean?

What about things that came out around the same time?—'Tommy' came out in '69, you were writing it in '67/68 I suppose, what did you think of things like 'Pet Sounds' by the Beach Boys, and 'Sgt. Pepper' from the Beatles?

Well, I thought they were amazing. In those days we were produced by Kit Lambert, and going to the studio was something to be sort of looked forward to and dreaded simultaneously, and I always saw 'Sgt. Pepper' and 'Pet Sounds' as being sort of group productions, if you like, by groups.

They seem to stand out, I mean as you say, the group suddenly say "we've been doing this job, now we'll do our thing". You know, the Beach Boys were getting into spiritual things . . .

Well, I think the thing about both of them that still amazes me to this day, is the fact that both of them have very loose concepts, and in a way the concept of 'Sgt. Pepper' is even looser than 'Pet Sounds', because they're both such amazing albums, and they both contain such incredible songs, a single sort of universal concept breathes through, that sort of oneness that comes from anything great. It's like looking at a great picture, or hearing a great piece of music.

At the time it came out I thought that Sgt. Pepper was almost great music but not quite. Now I think there is no doubt, it's amazing. But it was always an L.S.D. record to me.

It wasn't to me. I still get new things from it now. I think the thing about it was that it was so perfect that you couldn't believe it, and because it is practically perfect it will stay that way for centuries, and centuries and centuries. And I think the same thing applies to 'Pet Sounds'; and 'Pet Sounds' is a mono album, as well.

It's not really a concept album, it's just songs, isn't it?

No, it's the concept of making a perfect album, going so far that you're really trying to get perfection. It's something that the Who have never, ever done—I really got into the albums, but at the same time I still had had my basic sort of roots, which were based in all kinds of strange things. I realised the other day for example how much my writing was influenced by Mose Allison.

Didn't you try to do that even with 'Quadrophenia'?

No, not really. 'Quadrophenia' was slightly different, it was me trying to see if I could make an album with the Who which I controlled, that was all. I mean if I had been into making the perfect album I wouldn't have put it out because I knew when we were putting it out that it lacked dynamics.

I think that the great thing about the film was it revealed to me that 'Tommy' was still

very much alive, still evolving. I mean if you take something more recent like 'Quadrophenia' the day that that tape was delivered to MCA Records it was dead, from an evolutionary point of view. It was a statement made and isolated. There's a difference between something like that and something like 'Tommy' because 'Tommy' is evolving and sort of living, so you don't mind if it changes a little bit here and there because it still feels like it's working. That's what I feel about the distinction between something like 'I Can See For Miles' which is a statement made and finished and you either take it or leave it, and something like 'My Generation' which I think is still alive. I don't think it's a better record and I don't think it's a better song but it's better because it's still living.

I remember when you were mixing 'Quadrophenia' you kept going on about, this should be done again, and that's not right, and that's not right and should be redone . . . but you said that obviously you've got to stop somewhere and get on mixing. Whereas the Beach Boys' with that song 'Heroes and Villains' took about 9 months, or something, to do.

Well, yes. I've got thoughts about doing it now, doing a solo album, just 15 minutes a side, but perfect. Then I think, well, that's not really what it's all about. It's how precious you want to be, and what the right result is. I mean these are the times when preciousness in a way is important. The other thing about 'Quadrophenia' which makes it very distinctive to me in a sense, and it got misconstrued in a lot of ways, that it was in that sort of ilk and now we can be prepared for more albums like 'Quadrophenia' and 'Tommy'; it was really a grand flourish to tie up all the loose ends of the Who's obsessive thing with adolescence and rock and roll, which with people like Roger is still not dead, you know, but it's dead in me. I'm just not interested in punks on the street anymore, I'm not interested in baggy white trousers, and kids with their hair cut off. I'm too old for it, and I just wanted to—in one big fell swoop—build Jimmy up into this big sort of super-hero and then flop him down and leave him where we are today, fully illustrating the complete emptiness of the whole thing. And that's why it's not a particularly pleasant trip, in a way it's a very miserable sort of frustrated story. But I think it was important to do. I now feel good about the possibilities of future albums. I think the Who could do an album of 'Moon in June' songs now, but I'm not sure that my fans would see it the same way.

What did you think about people saying that 'Tommy' was influenced by 'S. F. Sorrow'!

Bullshit. I've heard 'S. F. Sorrow', but I actually heart it after 'Tommy' anyway.

And there was this thing of this 'Teenage Opera' with Keith West that they kept talking about, and they released a couple of singles.

I think they were quite good. In fact, I know the story, which was that I'd gone in the papers and I'd talked about doing this opera, and they just got fed up with waiting. In fact in two of his interviews he said that they'd got fed up with waiting for Pete Townshend's opera and gone and got on with making one. They never finished it though.

But really, it's all very well for me to be influenced by things, but I'm never influenced by anything that's going around now, never, not by the Stones or the Beatles or anybody. I was influenced by that music that we used to listen to in Ealing, and that's what formed my mind, and that was all my credentials for the way that I compose and stuff like that. And obviously a fantastic amount by Dylan, without understanding a fucking thing he was talking about or saying, he still gave me an incredible amount.

To get back to 'Tommy', in the original script a lot of it is this thing called 'Deceived' —a whole section, which as far as I can read in the script was lots of different short scenes. It was a very political thing, wasn't it? It was dropped. Now that would have changed Ken Russell's film quite a lot from your original 'Tommy' wouldn't it?

Yeah. I think basically the reason he took that out was because of Roger. Roger never liked the song and never, ever liked the idea of having it in. He thought it was too long and drawn out. I think it would have changed it a bit. All the additional bits that I've written in the thing have been written because Ken was worried that certain points might escape people, and if you look at them they're all heavily laden with information; like there's the bit towards the end where

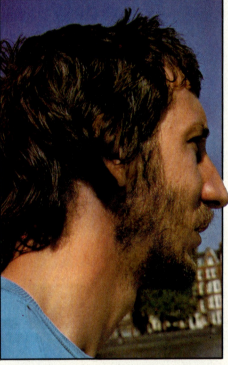

Frank and Nora are in a T.V. studio and they're sort of laying it on about the mother being genuine and sincere and wanting her son. She really believes her son is a great man and she wants to allow everybody to share in him, and Frank is saying "A Tommy camp in every city, but who am I to upset their plans, it could make a million", really laying Uncle Ernie on the line very clearly. And at the beginning of 'Amazing Journey' it's not "Deaf, dumb and blind boy" it's "Now he is deaf, now he is dumb, now he is blind", in case anybody's missed the point It's really so that people who only go and see the film once get the full impact of it, and I think 'Deceived' was something that Ken felt was important to get across the whole idea that the film of 'Tommy' had a political angle. But towards the end he figured it wasn't really necessary. In other words it was something which came through when you listened to 'Tommy', that it had a political thing which was never really specified, in the way that the drug thing was specified and the spiritual thing was specified and the child adolescent thing was specified. But the political social thing wasn't really clearly laid out, and I think he wanted to lay out the whole thing about the post war generation, which comes across a little bit in 'Sally Simpson'; that thing about a kid arguing with her parents about wanting to get into some sort of trip and they say "No, it's not going to be good for you" but at the same time saying things which in essence are very wise and true, which is one of the things which is so awful about your parents. On the one hand they're so stupid and on the other hand they're always so right, and that's very irritating.

But it was very political wasn't it? I got that impression reading it. People just walk out of their jobs to follow Tommy and lay down their tools to follow Tommy, and soldiers walk away from the parade ground, bank tellers walk out from behind the counter, production workers . . . all that sort of thing.

Well the idea of it was that Tommy was giving a lecture somewhere and Uncle Ernie was piping it through all the broadcast systems to the outside world, when he was just talking to a small band of people. It was to emphasise how the thing got out of scale.

About how Uncle Ernie was exploiting Tommy?

Yeah.

And it was dropped. Actually, in terms of making a film it was probably a good idea that it was dropped because it was so difficult and involved.

I didn't really ever like the piece of music written for it; Roger never liked it.

You recorded it?

Yeah. I liked bits of it.

Who sang it?

Roger sang it. It was on the tune of 'I'm Free', and it had bits of 'Sensation' in it.

It's called 'Deceived', it's obvious that the followers, the converts feel deceived by 'Tommy'.

No, no. It was "we've been deceived" . . .

What, by society?

Yeah. Basically the thing was that it was all supposed to be like post war, the war had just gone over and was being celebrated in a way, capitalism was taking root on the strength of the war and all this type of thing, or becoming strong on the strength of the war. Tommy was just saying that war is bad and it's all absurd because he could see bigger things above it all. In a way I'm glad that it's not in because I always felt that Tommy's trip towards the end was that he realised that the best thing for people to do was just carry on with their normal lives. It always worried me a bit.

Did it ever occur to you when Ken Russell wanted to make the film that he would just use it as a vehicle for his own point of view?

Well, I always felt that this was one of the most important things. When we first finished 'Tommy' we talked a lot about Ken Russell, and I liked the idea of Ken Russell because in those days he was a sort of arty film maker. It was only in more recent years that he started to get into things which are more sort of ego manifest. Then we went through a thing when what we were really after was a deal which would enable us to control the film. But we could never get close enough to that. Film companies would always want somebody else to control it really. And then in the end in frustration, because we so badly wanted the film to get made, we were almost going to take anybody that came along. We were involved in some talks with Hammer films and Hammer films mentioned Ken Russell, and I thought how amazing it would be if he would do it because he would make it his own, and I wouldn't have to sit there and explain it all. I mean the great thing about somebody like Ken Russell is he would stand by his own work. I just felt that he was a big enough character to take it and work with it. Also, I had a feeling that he would make a very good film because I do like a lot of his stuff that lots of other people don't necessarily like. Like I really like the 'The Music Lovers', and 'The Savage Messiah' and 'Mahler'.

If I had ever dug in my heels about 'Tommy' and said no-one has the right to change my conception, it would have killed 'Tommy' dead as a concept. A dead classic. I felt it was still evolving, still unfinished and still alive. I deliberately allowed it to become public domain to a point so it would stay alive. That was why when a ballet company or a college came on and asked permission to do their interpretation we gave them the go ahead. Once you start to be nit-picking about the rights of this and that, everything gets bogged down and the usual result is that the work dies of asphyxiation. In the case of Lou Reisner's 'Tommy' it was the idea of doing the production with a full orchestra that appealed to me—it had never been performed before to anything other than the Who's music. With Ken Russell I was prepared to make concessions and compromise some points in order to have Ken make his alterations—it just meant another evolution in the concept. I told him I didn't care if he altered all the words if he needed to: "Listening to you I get the porridge"—whatever he wanted. I used to be asked a lot of questions about what 'Tommy' meant which should be obvious after seeing the film. I don't think that rock and roll is something that Ken really cares intensely about or understands. He is interested in the phenomenon of rock and roll because it produces good ideas and some good music and he was interested in the spiritual implications of 'Tommy'. He is a very English director in as much as he really understood some of the early wartime sequences which I am sure no foreign director could have faithfully interpreted and he really has clarified the story line.

Do you like what he's done?

Yeah. I do. I think a lot of it falls short of the kind of technical camera excellence that is in a film like 'Mahler' or 'Savage Messiah', but then I think a lot of that would be out of place in 'Tommy'. I don't think 'Tommy' is really about great camera work or stimulating shots; I think it's about a story and I also think that the most important thing really is that 'Tommy' had quite a few sort of humorous angles about it, which have come across quite well.

Oliver Reed comes out of it very well.

Yeah. I think everybody comes out of it well. For example, the original doctor song was supposed to be tongue in cheek, which was never really grasped by anybody. In any of the remakes that were done of it, it was always treated very seriously. But you look at the words, they're such a joke. What are the lines in it? "He smiles, he cries, he pokes his tongue out at everyone" or something like that. It was meant to be fairly light-hearted, because it lays it on thicker about Tommy's remoteness.

Would you have liked 'Tommy' to have been made more as a rock film? The pinball wizard sequence is obviously like a rock film. It's a very exciting part. But something like the specialist is very formal and normal.

When we were mixing the album we realised that stuff like 'Holiday Camp' and 'Mother And Son' and stuff like that are very sort of like Ann-Margretty, you know, they're very sort of middle of the road music. It hasn't really worried me very much. I mean, if I had done the thing I think there's no doubt I would have tried to have made it more sort of rock universal, but then I don't think it would have worked properly because 'Tommy' isn't really bound in by that type of thing.

Has it occured to you that maybe the original Tommy rock concept has been made into a Mary Poppins? Maybe 'Who' fans will think that you've sold out.

It's occurred to me, yes. I think to a great degree you've got to live with the fact that it *has* been sold out. It's just that it should have been sold out sooner.

I don't mean anything against Ken Russell, I think he's done it well, but what I mean is that they might expect you to get some sort of 'acid-rock' film director to make it with 'acid-rock' people.

I don't know, it doesn't bother . . . I

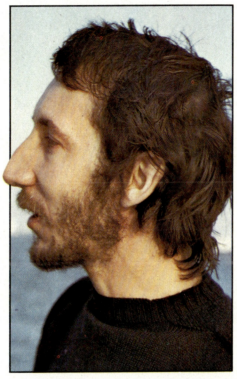

resisted all the legitimate actors in it. I resisted them all. I didn't want Ann-Margret in it. I didn't want Jack Nicholson and I didn't want Oliver Reed in it, because none of them were rock people and I wanted people that could sing rock—it was Ken who said that he had to have those people. He had to have people that could act and, if you like, Oliver Reed and Ann-Margret are the key people in it, they are the fundamental pivot of the film. I mean, the fact that Ann-Margret was a good singer was convenient and the fact that she wasn't a rock-type singer didn't matter too much because what we were really interested in was that fact that happens to be one of the only good actresses that can sing at all. In her class she's a great singer, you know, she's not necessarily entirely suited to rock but . . .

Who would you have cast in the different roles?

I made all kinds of suggestions in the beginning, I had a really crazy cast list. I wanted Tiny Tim as the Pinball Wizard because I imagined that it would sound really great on a hundred ukeleles. I just thought he was freaky enough and would be pretty good at it. I wanted Arthur Brown for the Doctor. I thought that the Mother would be good by a sort of older jazz singer who could sing rock, like Cleo Laine or Georgia Brown or somebody of that ilk, or maybe even somebody like Joan Baez.

Somebody said you wanted, or you were thinking of Stevie Wonder, is that right?

Well, this is a really awful story because Stevie Wonder was offered the part of Pinball Wizard by Robert Stigwood and I think was interested in doing it. Then Ken said you can't have a blind negro being beaten by a deaf dumb and white kid, because, well, it's just racially wrong. When the news got back to Stevie Wonder he was incredibly annoyed. When he came over to England, Eric Clapton and I went to see him and he wouldn't talk to us. He wouldn't talk to Eric at all because I was with Eric, and Eric couldn't work out what was going on. But when Eric saw him again in America he was really nice to him.

You think you got the blame? I heard somebody say Mick Jagger was approached.

Mick Jagger was considered for all kinds of things. He was adamant right from the very first time I spoke to him that he didn't want anything to do with it at all, but Robert Stigwood kept pushing and pushing. David Bowie we approached with the possibility that he might be interested in doing Pinball Wizard or Acid Queen. The same with Mick Jagger. And also we were talking about people like Lou Reed for Acid Queen. I wanted it to be more surreal, more sort of Fellini.

Who thought of Tina Turner?

Robert Stigwood.

She's very well cast. Why did Robert Stigwood produce it, was it his idea?

Yeah. I should think so. I think the thing is that he's had experience with making films of rock operas before. He knows that they work and that they make money in the shape of 'Jesus Christ Superstar'. He's an entrepreneur, and he's got plenty of money. He's always been a great friend of the group and of Kit and Chris—he's got an involvement. And through my involvement with Eric (Stigwood manages Eric Clapton) we were in contact with him at that time. I think it generally followed through. I don't know—I think there are a lot of things wrong with the way Stigwood goes about things, but I think in a way he's ideal for this type of thing because he's the kind of guy that really leaves people alone. Like he hasn't bothered Ken with a lot of stipulations about this and that. All he wanted was a good set of marquee names. He wanted Jack Nicholson, Oliver Reed and Elton John. Columbia were very willing to distribute the picture whoever was in it. They are happier with bigger names obviously, but the the reason it's good to have big names and the reason it does affect distributors is I think because a name like Jack Nicholson now is even hotter than it was at the beginning of the year. There'll be a million people go to see the film just because Jack Nicholson's in it.

Do you think they'll be disappointed that he's only got a guest appearance?

Oh yeah, I think they'll be disappointed. I think the other thing you've got to realise is how many cultist fans Ann-Margret has. I mean they might not necessarily be disappointed at the amount that she's on, but they might be disappointed at the way she's portrayed.

In a way, Keith Moon (as Uncle Ernie)

comes over as quite loveable in the film: he's meant to be evil in the script but he comes over quite loveable.

No, he's not meant to be particularly evil. He was in the original script, but then that role was taken over by Frank. So Uncle Ernie becomes just like Frank's stooge. Everything that you now see Oliver Reed doing in the film Keith was originally going to do. I mean all that the Lover was going to do in the original script was sit there looking loveable in the shape of Richard Chamberlain, and Tommy Steele was on the cards at one point to be the Lover.

Wasn't David Essex supposed to have been in it as well?

Ken Russell wanted David Essex in it, which was very weird because everyone else was against. I like him as a bloke, and I really feel bad about the fact that he was ever suggested and did the work that he did and was then turned down, because I don't like the way it reflects on me. Because we are good friends. And I like what he does in its way, and I really liked him the first time I saw him in 'Godspell', I thought he was fucking great in that. I think what he does is fairly lukewarm-alright. It doesn't worry me that much. Ken was just hyped up by the producer of 'Stardust', David Puttnam, by what went on when they were doing 'Stardust' up at Manchester Bellevue—5,000 little stupid teenyboppers storming the stadium.

When this film first started you seemed very unhappy. Unhappy is the politest word I could think of. In fact you disappeared for a bit. I always thought something must have gone down between Ken Russell and you or something, or were you just not happy with the way it was going?

I don't really know—this is something that happens to me often. People come up to me and say "Ah, it's really nice to know that you've got out of a bad scene", and I never know what they're talking about. All I really know is that I got dragged very low by the amount that I was drinking and by the fact that I was like . . . well, I was away from home and it was a sort of very low level of existence. That's really one of the things that puts me off touring—what everybody else in the band likes, getting pissed and going out. It makes me feel really awful because I feel generally sort of high and content just here doing nothing, just being what I am. All that seems to me to be throwing myself into what I regard as, not decadent, but sort of mucky and nasty. I mean I do like getting drunk, but it always makes me a wee bit depressed. I don't know why—I suppose because I'm sort of prudish about it and I don't like to . . . I feel sort of Christian about it you know—immoral.

There was a point when I was a bit peeved and that was when the filming first started at Harefield Grove. That pissed me off a bit because I didn't know quite what my role was, as this Musical Director, whereas in the studio I'd been working and effervescing. I used to roll up there at 8.30 and sit there all day—I can't say that that side of the film business did much for me.

You said to me once, after 'Tommy' this was, that when you're on stage you play your best, and you focus on Baba, you're playing to Baba on stage. Do you imagine that he's sitting in the audience, or sort of standing on stage?

Well he sort of constantly comes into my head on stage; it's like in any extreme, troubled situation, which is really what being on the stage is. I mean it's very nerve-racking.

It's great to be in a band like the Who because you could get away with anything—you can go on and be really terrible and yet still feel safe because you're not stuck out there on your own, you're contained within the aura of a group with a history and an image.

But it's still very nerve-racking and it's because it's such a strained situation that you tend to think of something that gives you comfort. You think of Baba. It doesn't happen quite so much now I must admit; in the last couple of tours that we've done I've been really disenchanted with playing on the stage, I just don't get anything out of it. I don't think there's any way to make it happen other than in a natural way and I think that what always used to give me great stamina and enthusiasm was the fact that 'Tommy' was a great vehicle and that always made me think of Baba all the time. I'd have him in the forefront, not subconsciously, but in the forefront of my imagination right the way through the performance. I think the Sundowner (Christmas 1973 gigs in London), apart from the gig we did at

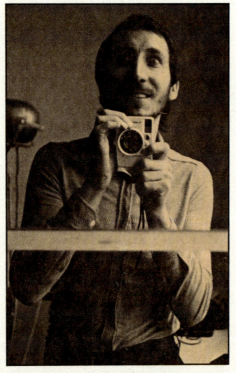

Portsmouth for the kids who did the film there, was the last really good gig that we did. The one at Portsmouth that we did for those kids was really amazing. The one at Charlton and the ones in America were absolute garbage, they really were so bad. Not manifestly, I mean they could be quite good, in a way, or above avergae. But there was really no magic in them for me, they were very bland. I thought perhaps a lot of it might have been my fault in a way, I was so fully occupied in other things.

But I think one thing that might be nice—a nice bonus from the 'Tommy' film—is that it might enable us to justify playing more of it on stage again. I mean you don't often come up with numbers that are as ballsy as 'I'm Free. . . .

But then again the audience always want it, don't they? I always felt that the Who was fed up with 'Tommy' and although the audience wanted it the Who had had enough of it.

That was very true. I mean we did play the whole thing all the time, and we were fed up with it.

It would be great if the Who got together and did the whole thing an as opera again. I don't know whether it's possible anymore. I mean is Moony capable of that? It must have taken a lot of bloody work—a lot of energy.

Yeah, it did. Moony's a better drummer now in fact, but . . . well, we're all a lot older. I mean, I find it a lot more difficult to prance about on the stage. If we're contemplating a six week tour I'm going to have to go into a gymnasium, because it really does take a lot out of you to play. It depends what length the show is: one and a half, one and three quarter hours is just about the length of a football match, and I think anybody can play football for one and a half hours and occasionally go into a spurt of energy, but the one that included 'Tommy' used to be three hours long.

I think that Ken Russell's film is going to sort of show a lot of people what 'Tommy' is about for the first time. What I think is so surprising is that Ken Russell has done such a literal translation of 'Tommy'. It got changed as he was doing it, a lot got changed, but the script seemed very literal.

Yes. This amazed me because I had always thought that probably one of the biggest mistakes the Who ever made, or maybe it was just me, was doing something as story-like as 'Tommy' and then explaining it as carefully as I did. Bob Dylan for example, never says anything about his songs and from odd things that he has said, he seems to have absolutely nothing to say. He really hasn't. It's like me in a way. If somebody asked me about 'Substitute' I wouldn't know really what to say because I didn't really write it, it just sort of emerged. And 'I Can See For Miles', I didn't really have a lot to do with at the time. And it wasn't because I was doped out of my brain or anything . . .

You don't sit down consciously and intellectually and think: "I will write a song about this"?

No. I was just in my little studio playing for amusement, and often I used to scribble out lyrics very quickly so that I'd have something to write and play around with. If you like, it's stream of consciousness stuff and I think Dylan's writing practically always seems to be like that—he consciously does it now; he goes into a studio and if they don't get it first time round he scraps the whole thing and a lot of the musicians who work with him can't get into that. I'm the reverse. I still write the same way, I still tend to write off the top of my head but once I've written it I don't see why I shouldn't cut it. Critics can talk about my stuff—why can't I? I just become my own critic and I analyse my own stuff. That's really what happened with 'Tommy', and I think it's quite good in a way that 'Tommy' has been able to stand that.

One very important thing about 'Tommy' I think, is that you haven't really—and this is a bit sad for people who never saw it—but you haven't really heard 'Tommy' or experienced it until you've seen it live. And then when you go back and listen to the record, although the record's got everything that the live performance has, it's just nowhere near the same—at all. This sounds like Roger Daltrey's thing, he's always going on about you've got to hear the Who live, but he's dead right.

But he also says other things which are based on that kind of thing—he says that you've got to allow things to emerge from a road situation, as 'Tommy' came from the road, and you've got to rehearse things before you go into a studio. You've got to play them on stage before you go into a studio. A lot of this type of thing did happen with 'Tommy'. But the thing that's different is that at that particular time we didn't know that much about recording. Kit Lambert was still learning and he didn't really produce to make a good sound. He produced to try and get the most difficult group to record a well-known record. And we've still got the same problem, we're still very, very difficult to record—not to make sound good but to get the excitement that is obviously in the band, across.

Look at that Charlton thing, you look at the T.V. thing and you see the group and you hear the music—and I did as good a mix as I could and I know the visuals aren't up to much—but because you're not there, the whole thing might just as well not happen. It just doesn't equal what actually happens out front at the concert. But there's no question in my mind that the Who will probably never reach that kind of peak we got during that performance of 'Tommy' because it was . . .

It was more than just a concert, it was a fascinating kind of experience.

Well it was for us. What was pushing us on was knowing that this was really doing us good and that it was really working, whereas most live performances of any group not least the Who, are 50% getting through and 50% frustration. The great thing about 'Tommy' was that it was 100% getting through.

I always watch audiences when I go to concerts, I find them fascinating. The most amazing I've ever seen was at a Beatles concert. This was when the Who were relatively unknown and got a couple of dates playing at the bottom of the bill on a Beatles concert in Blackpool in about 1964. I went along with the group and I watched the Beatles very closely from the side of the stage. The young girls in the audience were as interesting and exciting as the Beatles. All fainting and going into trances and screaming. Anyway another incredible audience reaction but very different, was when The Who played at the Isle of Wight festival. The Who just walked on and went straight into 'Tommy', all the way through about a thousand times better than the record. I hadn't seen The Who for about two years and I was amazed at how professional you were. I was sitting there in the very front row transfixed, and I looked around at the half a million people behind me and they were all transfixed too. Sitting there with their mouths open and trembling. That was a remarkable concert.

I remember your comment afterwards. You came back and said, "You know, you're quite good. You're developing into quite a nice little group".

What was incredible about the Isle of Wight thing was that the Who were totally and completely in control. We'd just come back from that lengthy American tour, and half way through that American tour we played at a place called Chicago Electric Kinetic theatre or something, Joe Cocker was on the bill, he'd done a whole tour with us. We'd open up with 'Can't Explain', 'Substitute' maybe even the 'Mini-Opera' and stuff like that, then we'd play 'Tommy' from start to finish, which was still bubbling about in the bottom of the American charts in the 50's, and then we'd finish up with 'My Generation' or something and a great big, long-drawn-out boogie including 'Magic Bus'. The heavy metal. The kids used to like the heavy metal, but they didn't know quite what to make of 'Tommy' and so people just used to sit very quietly and they wouldn't clap between numbers and they didn't know whether to be respectful or what because this was the Who who at the end of the act were going to smash up their instruments. They didn't know what was going to happen. Now half way through this gig in Chicago all of a sudden everybody realised that something was working—I don't know quite what it was but everybody all at the same time, just stood up and stayed standing up.

From that moment on they would always stand up at exactly this same point, and I could never work out—I can't remember when it was. It might have been 'Listening To You' or at the end of 'Go To The Mirror Boy'. It was the first time we'd created a theatrical device that worked every time. Like a piece of opera where when the heroine dies it always makes you feel a little bit sad. This was the first thing that really worked, apart from smashing guitars, every time. It was the first thing

that we could rely on. We really started to explore its potential so that by the time we got round to the Isle of Wight we knew exactly what worked and what you skipped over and got done quickly. It was a great concert for us, because we felt so in control of the whole situation. We were able to just come in, do it and not need to know anything about what was going on. In other words we didn't spend time at the Festival getting into the vibrations, didn't stay to see Bob Dylan, didn't care what was going on. We knew that stage act we had, with 'Tommy' in it, would work under any circumstances because it had worked so many times on the tour. I think that was a great part of that period for the Who, because we knew the instrinsic stage theatrical power of 'Tommy'. It was rock and roll, but it was still a piece of theatre that we knew worked, like Agatha Christie and 'The Mousetrap'. We knew it was going to have a long run. We knew we were on to a good thing and it gave us such strength and confidence. Now the Who are again back on the road looking for something new, I think we're back where we were 10 years ago. We're back again in exactly the same position.

But it must be quite exciting to be in that position?

Oh yes, it's nice to be able to afford to get into that. It's frustrating sometimes when people can't wait because they don't believe, if you like, in magic. They believe in facts. That's why sometimes it's very difficult for me to work things out effectively inside a group like the Who. 'Tommy' met up with so much group opposition at first.

Was that when you were writing it?

Yeah, you go on and on and on. They were fed up with the fact that it took so long to do.

But what did they think about it when you came and played them bits? Did they think "here he goes , , , he's got into this Eastern geezer, this mystical geezer and he's round the twist like all the others"? Because John wrote two numbers for it and they seem to fit in very well.

Well, we did talk about it a lot on the tour previous to the one I've just been talking about, I actually explained the idea to the group. Roger seemed to quite like the idea, Keith would always go along with whatever I suggested, and John quite liked the idea and was quite keen on writing something for it. But when we got into the studio to actually record it and it took months and months and months, they got very fed up with it. They got fed up with the fact that Kit and I were always rowing about it. Kit wanted the Who to do the backing tracks and bring in hundreds of fucking french horns and all that, and I was always fighting with him that we definitely mustn't do that.

Why, because you'd got to do it on the road or because it'd got to be the Who?

No, because it'd just got to be the Who. That's the way it always was, a sort of unwritten law with the band which I knew counted.

Did you ever think that 'Tommy' would ever be as successful as it is?

I don't know. I suppose I always hoped that it was going to be as big. I still can't credit the fact that six years after it was originally written it is still gaining strength. Obviously I've got this jaundiced point of view 'cos I know what went into it, but to me it's definitely got Baba's touch on it. It was the first thing I wrote, completed, and dedicated to Baba and thought about sincerely from a sort of spiritual point of view and to try and do some good etc . . . all these sort of bullshit Christian sort of standpoints, rather than adopting a cynical thing and being deliberately big headed and cuntish because I thought that was the way it was best to be. And suddenly everything was working and continues to work. Then I got drawn back into what the Who is, which is just four brats really, and I saw that as four brats they're quite successful because they've been going for such a long time, but 'Tommy' is the purest thing they've ever done, and it's still got this incredible momentum. It is making a film when the Who have been trying to make a film for years and years and years. So with all the Who's great record success and everything else, we haven't been able to do it on our own merit. But 'Tommy' has.

You're talking about just a film with the Who in it?

A film that the Who would make in the same way that the Who make a record, or

123

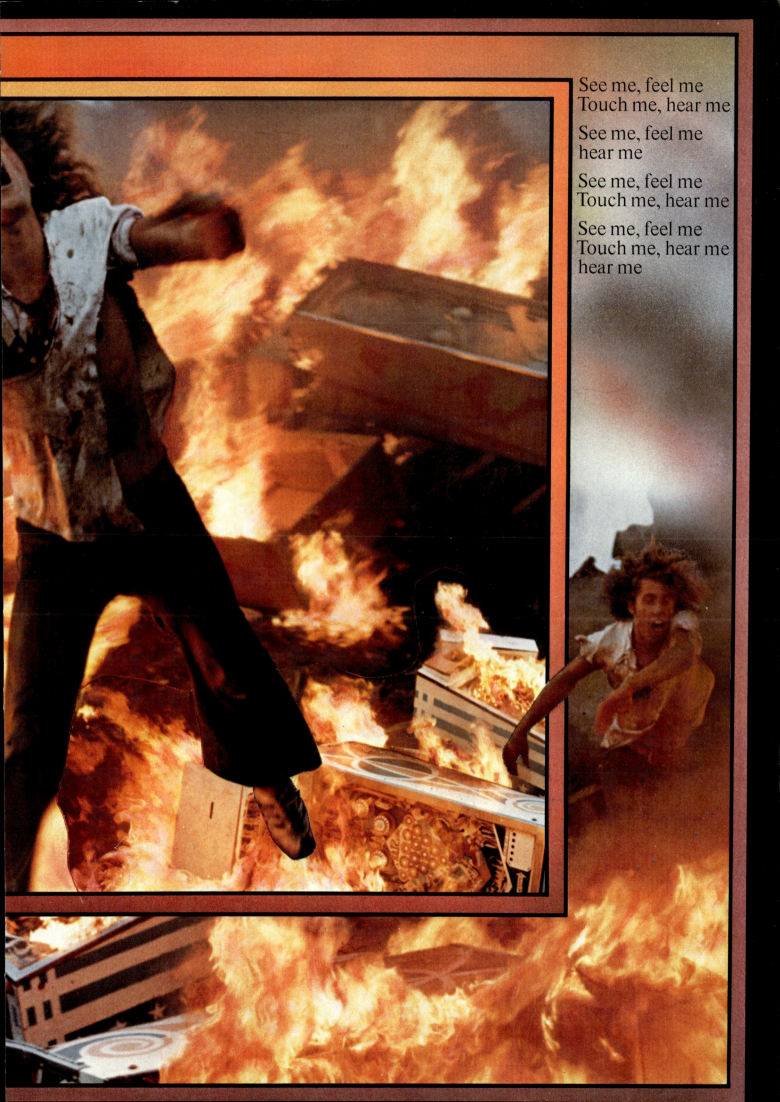

Listening to you I get the music
Gazing at you I get the heat
Following you I climb the mountain
I get excitement at your feet!
Right behind you I see the millions
On you I see the glory
From you I get opinions
From you I get the story

the way the Beatles made films.

Are you worried that 'Tommy's' going to get bigger than the Who?

I think it is already.

When it came out you got accepted by Leonard Bernstein and all sorts of very serious music people. That must have been very satisfying.

Well . . . for example there's a guy who writes in the Sunday Times called Derek Jewell and at the end of the year he picks all the albums where people have tried to do something daring—like he'll take Rick Wakeman album, a Yes album, and ELP album, maybe 'Quadrophenia' or something and 'Tubular Bells', and put them together and say "this is the new wave of rock symphonists, people who know how to use rock and take it on and in centuries to come rock and roll won't be understood but these works will be understood because they have musical form". I still have this feeling that the most important thing isn't musical form but all the fundamentals of rock and roll. That's what I still dig. And I still get something between the lines which has got nothing to do with music, nothing to do with the lyrics. I get very upset sometimes when I see people take a song like 'Summertime Blues' and then say the reason why it's great is because it's about Summertime or about driving my '57 Chevvy. It's just a great thing, and it underestimates it in a way to talk about it as music. And I mean I get very upset also when I see something like: "Pete Townshend and his own distinctive guitar—take the one note solo in 'I Can See For Miles' where he takes just one note and plays it, but that one note is worth every Eric Clapton solo . . . " type of thing. I played one note in it because I couldn't be bothered to play a solo, and it's horrible to hear everything analysed all for the wrong reasons.

All those people who intellectualise about pop, and I hope we ain't doing it, are sad anyway. I even heard the other day on Radio 3 they mathmatically analysed works of Beethoven and Debussy and all these people and they said 'this cadenza was exactly the same as used by Tchaikovsky in the opening of his so and so', and to them it's all movements and notes and patterns, very mathmatical and scientific. Rock and roll throws all that stuff out of the window, doesn't it?

But people are starting to get away with it now because inevitably a lot of those people, I don't think they're rock musicians, are starting to sell albums these days. Mike Oldfield and Rick Wakeman and even Yes, they're not rock groups by any stretch of the imagination. They're into sound and music and composition. But the thing with the Who is that its only embarkation into music proper, I think, was in the shape of 'Tommy'. Definitely one of the things that's great about an idea like 'Tommy', which makes music a great vehicle for an idea, is that if you like the music you can live with it over a much longer period of time because, for example, you like certain melodies. Say you like the way that 'Pinball Wizard' comes out at the end of side three or something, you sit through the whole of side three in order to get 'Pinball Wizard'. But then two years later you discover you're getting into something else about it, so then you listen to the whole album and then you discover something else. I think this is the thing, that music continues to evolve in the mind of the listener. I find this now with all kinds of music that I listen to. I get a completely different thing now from certain Dylan material, and also from lots of other stuff that I used to listen to, probably more from classical music and stuff like that. I find that by living with something for a long period of time you start to drop layer by layer, deeper and deeper into it until you sort of own it. The thing about music is that you can possess it, because it is just—it's infinitely recordable. It's very hard to fade an image in the mind's eye but it's quite easy to summon up a fragment of music that can bring back all the sort of impressions that you require.

There is that strange sort of emotional thing, or whatever it is, that incredible thing you get from great music that transcends just listening to a tune. I'm thinking mostly of classical music now, great music. It has that incredible sort of spiritual stirring quality of getting to something within you—some higher level within you. It's the only time when rugged hard men would use the

word "beauty" which they would normally think was sissy.

Yeah, and on the surface it probably isn't at all, but it just summons up that kind of amazing—I know what you mean. But there's been an awful shroud, and probably will remain so, over classical music—I mean all classical music is a collection of history's hits, and what is an awful veil over it is that it is now performed without any trace of emotion. It's like saying that today's orchestra is a Synthesiser and performing things that were meant to be performed on 5-string Irish lutes on a synthesiser, because the synthesiser gives a cleaner record production, or something like that. Thus equalising everything out. But that thing that you were saying about the valve that opens up, I get that feeling from a fantastic amount of rock music as well. I get that spiritual lift if you like, that peak of perfection through other things. It's much more difficult when a musical piece has got words because you tend to sort of follow the words and try and find some meaning in them, but there are certain fragments of 'Pet Sounds' or 'Sgt. Pepper' or high spots of the Stones like 'Satisfaction' and stuff like that. Well, for me that song that they did—'The Last Time'—is absolutely amazing. As soon as I hear that I immediately tend to be higher up than when I started off. And there are bits of Rachmaninoff, and the Mozart piece—the trio piece that they use in 'Sunday, Bloody Sunday'. There's a homosexual doctor who's having a love affair with this boy who's also having a love affair with a girl, and he's very remote and lonely because he's a homosexual, but every time you see him in his flat he's playing this trio from Mozart, which is a superbly beautiful piece of music. It justs lifts you whenever you see him you see through rose coloured spectacles, and you end up seeing this queer, fucked-up doctor like some sort of Marilyn Monroe figure, you know what I mean? Like 'Death in Venice', using that incredible piece of music throughout the whole film just to put that point across. Without those pieces of music, those films would not happen. There are certain things music can do which no film, no pictorial image, can ever do. It can't switch people up a stop in that automatic way. You take it to its most fundamental level, the classic things like 'You'll Never Walk Alone'—look what that does at a football match. People that I know that hate football say that they've gone to a football match and people have started singing 'You'll Never Walk Alone' and they've felt like they're at a Nazi rally. They've just got completely swept away with it. When it's finished and the football game starts they think 'what the hell have I been doing? I've lost myself in this universal massive human excrement'. Or whatever. You know—rugby songs. The fact that you lose yourself along the line. I don't quite know what it is. This is what always makes me laugh about the pomposity of classical music—all these Whitehouse-like old dears that put on bits of Handel's 'Messiah'. What they're really doing is freaking inside they're letting go. They're having a little trip. They're putting that record on, sitting there drinking their tea, and they're tripping out, really freaking—not outwardly, but it's all happening inside.

I've got George Harrison written down in my notes, but I don't know why. Probably because he was in a similar position to you in 1968 or when you were writing 'Tommy'. A rock musician getting into mysticism. I can't think of any others who were.

It was very unfashionable because dope, acid in particular, was still a happening thing. It made people interested in spiritual things, they kept taking the tablets, as it were, and interest just shifted all the time, from one thing to another. If you like, they missed the stop—they'd keep coming in and out of the railway station but not ever get off the train. I think where I was infinitely lucky, although when it comes to me being a viable advertising vehicle it's very bad for me to talk about it, was that I had such a terrifying trip. It really did make me push the whole thing away. If I hadn't had that really awful trip on that plane back from Monterey, I probably would still be into drugs. I found it very easy to accept what Baba said about drugs because it just seemed to happen that way. I actually felt physically damaged by it. That's why I never really feel I'm doing anything courageous or selfless by not involving myself in it. It was very easy to do.